CAREER AND MOTHERHOOD

CAREER AND MOTHERHOOD

Struggles for a New Identity

Alan Roland and **Barbara Harris**
with contributors

HUMAN SCIENCES PRESS
72 Fifth Avenue   3 Henrietta Street
NEW YORK, NY 10011 ● LONDON, WC2E 8LU

Library of Congress Catalog Number 78-8026

ISBN: 0-87705-372-3

Copyright © 1979 by Human Sciences Press
72 Fifth Avenue, New York, New York 10011

Printed in the United States of America
9 987654321

Library of Congress Cataloging in Publication Data

Roland, Alan, 1930-
    Career and motherhood.

    Includes index.
    1. Mothers—Employment—Social aspects—United States
—Addresses, essays, lectures.   2. Wives—Employment—
Social aspects—United States—Addresses, essays, lec-
tures.   3. Social role—Addresses, essays, lectures.
4. Identity (Psychology)—Addresses, essays, lectures.
I. Harris, Barbara, 1942-   joint author. II. Title.
HD6055.R64   331.4   78-8026
ISBN 0-87705-372-3

To our spouses and children:
Jackie and Joel;
and
Tika, Ariel, and Clifford

CONTRIBUTORS

Doris Bernstein, M.A.—President, Institute of Psychoanalytic Training and Research; Faculty Member,
I.P.T.A.R. and N.P.A.P. Paper published on "Childhood Identity Synthesis." In *Psychoanalytic Monographs I, Identity, Identification and Self-Image.* (Ed.)
Alan Roland, Ph.D.

Barbara Harris, Ph.D.—Professor of History, Pace U., and
a member of the Institute for Research in History.
Specialization in English and Women's History. Has
taught courses and published papers in both areas.
Author of *Beyond Her Sphere: Women and the Professions
in American History* to be published by Greenwood
Press in Fall 1978. Has participated in the C. Mil-
dred Thompson Memorial Symposium, Vassar College, 1975, on integrating women's history into the
introductory history course; in a program, "Images
of Women," sponsored by the Delaware Endow-

ment for the Humanities, 1975; and in a program entitled "Opportunities, Problems, and the Future for Women in Management," at Simpson College, 1976. Member of Columbia U. Seminar on Women and Society; Coordinating Committee of Women in the Historical Profession; and Research Groups on Women's History and on Family History and Demography.

Charlotte Kahn, Ed.D.—Psychoanalyst. Faculty, N.P.A.P. Associate Professor, Child and Family Studies; Director, Marriage and Family Counselling Program, College for Human Development, Syracuse University. Has published a variety of papers, including ones on creativity.

Jane Lazarre—Noted feminist writer. M.A. in anthropology. Articles on feminism and psychoanalysis and other topics in *The Village Voice, Ms., Viva,* and other publications. Author of *The Mother Knot,* and of *On Loving Men* to be published by Dial Press in Spring 1979. Teaches women's studies at City College of New York.

Esther Menaker, Ph.D.—Faculty, N.Y.U. Postdoctoral Program in Psychoanalysis and N.P.A.P. Author of seminal papers on masochism and the self. Co-author of *Ego in Evolution.* Manuscript in progress, on Otto Rank. Author of "The Therapy of Women in the Light of Psychoanalytic Theory and the Emergence of a New View." In *Women in Therapy.*

Harriette Podhoretz, Ph.D.—Psychoanalyst. Faculty, N.P.A.P. and the N.J. Center for Psychoanalysis. Ph.D. dissertation on women who have doctorates.

Alan Roland, Ph.D.—Faculty, N.P.A.P. and the Center for Expressive Analysis. Formerly Director of the Institute and Program Chairman, N.P.A.P.; Instructor, The New School, in course on Identity and Self-Image, and an interdisciplinary course integrating psychoanalysis with sociology, anthropology, and history. Various papers published in the *International Journal of Psychoanalysis* and *The Psychoanalytic Review* on psychoanalytic technique, dream interpretation, and psychoanalytic literary criticism. Contributor and editor of *Psychoanalytic Monographs I, Identity, Identification, and Self-Image.* Contributor and editor of *Psychoanalysis, Creativity and Literature: A French-American Inquiry.* Columbia U. Press, 1978. Senior Research Fellow, American Institute of Indian Studies; "Identity Conflicts and Resolutions in Urban India," 1977–78.

CONTENTS

9

PREFACE

Barbara Seaman

Few of us have the courage to take a stance against our culture. Most of us are heavily influenced by the prevailing social beliefs of our time.

From the 1830's until the 1960's, motherhood, in the United States, was considered a full-time job. In fact, this point of view was eccentric. Anthropologists and historians agree that in a majority of cultures—and even in ours before the Industrial Revolution—parenting was a function to be shared by mother, father, extended family, persons too old for heavy work, siblings, or professionals with certain skills to whom a child might be apprenticed for income or study.

It is illuminating to read the "Last Will and Testament" of Dr. Samuel Fuller, who came to Plymouth Colony on the Mayflower, and was our first physician. Fuller had in his charge several children, including females, who were not his own. Apparently they showed an early aptitude in medicine or midwifery, which his wife, Mistress Bridget Fuller, practiced. At the same time, one of the Fuller's own children was not a member of their household. She boarded elsewhere, perhaps because she did not have the healing vocation. With the Industrial Revolution, the separation of home and work, came The Cult of Domesticity—or True Womanhood—which historian Barbara Harris describes. Of course, there were still mothers who worked outside the home, but the ideal in this country for some 130 years was to be a fulltime mother and manager of one's own children. Most women who opted for serious careers forewent motherhood, and even marriage. What had happened was that economic realities, the father's daily separation from his family, the mother's separation from remunerative work, dictated a new "psychology" of childcare.

As The Cult of True Womanhood descended upon us, Elizabeth Cady Stanton beamed her powerful intellect on trying to fend it off. Her large and happy family helped to carry on her work. While Mrs. Stanton is best remembered for her women's suffrage campaign, she also wrote brilliant and impassioned commentaries against the self-appointed childcare authorities of her time. These writings interwove the personal and the political. Dr. Harris' essay, "Two Lives, One Twenty-Four Hour Day," is much in the Stanton tradition.

We are in a generation where our concepts of womanhood—and manhood—are changing convulsively. Psychoanalyst Alan Roland is understating when he observes: "... perhaps one can go so far as to say that any educated woman of today must consider the option of a dual-role identity of career and motherhood.... it is rare to have new identity integrations occur without the arousal of anxiety, guilt and conflict."

Readers who consider such psychoanalytic observations to be "soft" might look at the new birth statistics. The age of first-time motherhood, at least in select groups, is rising dramatically. Women of intellect or ambition are completing their education, establishing themselves in their professions, and, only then, giving birth to a first child. A "significant cohort," as the demographers put it, is delaying motherhood until the late 20's and 30's, even though obstetrics textbooks continue to define a mother who has her first child after age 30 as an "elderly primapara."

I started by noting that we cannot confront our culture lightly. We are buffeted by it in ways we do not discern. Motherhood as a full-time job was an historical expedient, now becoming obsolete. This is not a value judgment but a statement of fact. At present, only seven out of one hundred United States households include a working father, children, and an unemployed wife!

Development experts no longer claim that the children of working mothers are destined to have more problems than those of full-time homemakers. Yet, children still need love and supervision. Alternative solutions for affordable, quality childcare have not yet been established in our country. Today's working mother is almost bound to feel uneasy, partly because of the scarcity of mother substitutes, and partly because of the conflicts Dr. Roland and his colleagues describe. It's true that we have new options, but we cannot entirely escape parental values. Hence, the concept of identity struggle, as formulated by the contributors to this book, should supply invaluable insights to the mothers of our transitional generation. At one point in my own life I entered a consciousness-raising group for writer-mothers. The material which emerged was so painful that after four or five sessions we agreed to terminate. All of us were feminists and alumnae of other such women's groups, but with a broader focus. Jane Lazarre's essay brought those motherhood meetings back, in a rush of emotion. One woman, a distinguished novelist, had observed, "The way you spell motherhood is G-U-I-L-T."

I believe that this book will help us begin to dissipate the guilt and conflict we working mothers are all bound to feel. In *Career and Motherhood,* the reader will find a treasured counsellor—and friend.

INTRODUCTION

Social change is the idiom of the modern era. Perhaps in no other area of contemporary American society has social change been so rapid and far-reaching as women's roles, attitudes, and self-awareness. One of the most vital aspects of these sweeping changes involves an increasing number of women who are striving to combine serious career commitments with marriage and raising a family. It has not always been this way. Nor do all women now choose such a dual-role identity of career and motherhood. Many select the more traditional role of homemaker, while some concentrate on a career, either with or without marriage, and without children. But one can say that any educated, modern young woman must consider the option of a dual-role identity of career and motherhood.

To forge this new dual-role identity, women often struggle on three different fronts. On the broad social one, they frequently encounter attitudes and role expectations at variance with their life-style, not to mention innumerable practical difficulties. Achieving a dual role also results in considerable reverberations within the family, posing challenges to the role and identity of their husbands—a situation that does not always end in an amicable resolution. More than one divorce has resulted from the stresses and strains involved in changing family roles. On a profound inner level are the psychological conflicts often engendered by this new identity. It is rare to have new identity integrations occur without the arousal of anxiety, guilt, and conflict.

To state that these women's difficulties and conflicts in achieving career, marriage, and motherhood are simply a result of current cultural attitudes and roles and past psychological conditioning is a not infrequent cliché. It unfortunately begs the question of more searching sociohistorical and psychological analyses. For example, current social mores derive from historical traditions and operate within certain contemporary social structures. Conditioning, on the other hand, is a rather simplistic concept covering a complexity of processes involving the conscious and unconscious internalization of social reality within the varied familial relationships of childhood and adolescence. Some of these internalizations are highly relevant to later struggles with career and motherhood. Moreover, conditioning, a concept of behavioral psychology, implies a mechanistic view of humans as objects easily manipulated without either conscious will or unconscious motivation—not so dissimilar from the animal in laboratory experiments where the concept of conditioning originally derived. We hope to present here a far more humanistic and complex view of human nature, one rooted in social and historical reality.

This book delves into women's struggles to achieve a dual-role identity of career and motherhood on different related levels: the sociohistorical level, involving the effects of historical traditions and forces on current social patterns, roles, and attitudes, including the practical arrangements that have to be made for the functional realization of a dual-role identity; and the psychological level. The psychological dimension in particular calls for a reformulation of the psychoanalytic psychology of women, one that focuses much more on issues of self and identity than classical psychoanalysis, which has tended to be male-oriented. Moreover, any considerations in the psychology of women necessarily have implications for certain aspects of the psychology of men, particularly in respect to their relationships with women and children. Furthermore, any new psychoanalytic formulations around these issues must be integrated within the broader sociohistorical framework. Our approach, therefore, must ultimately be interdisciplinary.

These different levels will be explored by women specialists from different disciplines. A cogent question may have already occurred in the reader's mind: Why is a man involved in organizing this book, writing the introduction and initial theoretical chapter, and collaborating on the concluding chapter? The answer is simple, but to answer it fully requires becoming personal—something easy to do on this subject. As women strive for a dual-role identity, men are inevitably drawn into the vortex of social change. In effect, we are writing about a subject in which we are all intrinsically involved—participant observers[1] in the flux of contemporary social change. Men are obviously integral to women's achieving career and motherhood in their roles as husbands, lovers, and fathers; they are equally central to the attitudes and options of the next generation of women and men. Men simply cannot be considered apart from this whole social process.

[1]Harry Stack Sullivan used this phrase to describe the role of the psychoanalyst, but it seems equally pertinent to our subject here, especially if "participant" is underlined.

More personally, my wife and I married when she was in the middle of a doctoral program in Middle Eastern history and I was working as a clinical psychologist and was in psychoanalytic training. By the time we had children, we were both firmly rooted in our respective careers. As my wife continued her career as a history professor, it became apparent that there are many many different dimensions and levels to the problems and adjustments involved in her and other women's combining their careers with families— not to mention the husbands. In fact, for a period of a few years there was hardly a dinner party or social event where the subject did not come up in prolonged and intense discussion. Common struggles appeared as couples went through the same experience. Serious strains sometimes developed in relationships with older couples where the wife had given up career aspirations to stay home with the children. Expressions of guilt were at times rampant.

Certain aspects of these common struggles were not readily understandable and cried out for depth psychological analysis. Yet psychoanalytic theory as usually formulated seemed inadequate to the task. My psychoanalytic curiosity became more and more aroused about the nature of the unconscious factors involved in the problems and conflicts of women and men struggling to achieve this new life-style. It was also apparent that an increasing number of my women patients were struggling to work out similar problems in career and love relationships that also needed elucidation. Sometimes, for example, love relationships or motherhood were experienced as distinct threats to career involvement and were therefore shunned. In retrospect, I have found that as a result of working on this subject, subtle conflicts in women patients involving career, love relationships, and motherhood have become much clearer and therefore much easier to resolve.

As Co-Chairperson of Scientific Programs at the National Psychological Association for Psychoanalysis

(N.P.A.P.),[2] I decided to explore the subject in a scientific meeting. I turned to some of my women colleagues, who themselves combined a dual-role identity of career and motherhood and who had given a great deal of thought to the subject. I had already realized that many of the traditional Freudian psychoanalytic views on women were seriously wanting, and new formulations were badly needed. My departure from classical psychoanalysis on this subject was undoubtedly influenced by being trained in the nonmedical psychoanalytic movement in New York City, in good part by women analysts. Here, one's psychoanalytic identity and viewpoint do not have to be part of the psychoanalytic establishment, and women analysts are clearly as influential as the men.

In organizing such a program, I knew from my own work on identity and the self that it was essential to incorporate a strong sociohistorical view to provide the context for psychoanalytic insights, and to present this dimension in its own right. In short, an interdisciplinary approach was the only way of tackling this subject. Professor Barbara Harris, a historian who had already done considerable research on women with professional and other career interests in the United States, presented a paper, an expanded version of which appears as Chapter 3 in this book. Later I invited her to edit the book with me. Not only does she provide the necessary perspective of a woman for such a book but, equally important, her mastery of the social and historical literature on women is crucial for a true integration with the psychoanalytic dimension. We have coauthored the concluding chapter, and have attempted to

[2]The N.P.A.P. is the largest of the nonmedical psychoanalytic institutes, with approximately 40% of its members and faculty being women —a sharp contrast to the American Psychoanalytic Association, where only 4% are women, although many women have played a major role in the organization.

integrate the sociohistorical with the psychoanalytic in discussing dual-role identity—something that is impossible for psychoanalyst or historian to do alone.

I further realized from several years of participation in an etching workshop[3] with a number of professional women artists that women who are artists and mothers have unique problems in their dual-role identities. I therefore invited Jane Lazarre—a noted feminist writer sophisticated in psychoanalysis, and author of *The Mother Knot,* a book on motherhood—to present these problems at the meeting and, of course, later to contribute to this book.

The meeting, entitled "The Professional Woman and Mother: Problems of a New Identity," was held in January 1976 during the worst blizzard of that winter. Despite the snowstorm, it was extremely well-attended. At none of the other 40 or more scientific meetings that I have organized and chaired for the National Psychological Association for Psychoanalysis, nor any that I have attended elsewhere, have I heard both panelists and audience deal with a subject on such an emotional and personal level. There were considerable attempts to give the subject a shape, form, and conceptual understanding. But this was always punctuated by references to personal experiences in the present and in childhood. Psychoanalysts rarely become this open. It became obvious that everyone was trying to grope for and understand the effects of crucial factors in their own lives related to dual-role identity in women, and the effects of dual-role identity on the roles and identities of the husband-father. It was also apparent that for some women negotiating this new identity was much easier than for others. The response to the meeting was highly enthusiastic, and it was clear that the subject warranted expansion and elaboration into a book.

[3]The Ruth Leaf Etching Workshop in Douglaston, Queens.

The book begins in a down-to-earth manner by exploring the innumerable everyday practical arrangements and difficulties that women must cope with in implementing a dual-role identity of career and motherhood. Barbara Harris draws extensively on her own experiences, as well as those of a number of other women, in writing "Two Lives, One 24-Hour Day." This chapter takes into account various social forces involving career and motherhood, and forms a practical context for the succeeding chapters.

The next issue concerns the kind of theoretical framework which could encompass such diverse levels as the everyday struggles with current social reality, the legacy of historical attitudes, roles, and institutions, and the dynamic, unconscious, emotional factors. It seemed to me that the concept of identity could explicitly and implicitly include all of these dimensions. Erik Erikson, who undoubtedly did more than anyone to develop this concept, is a psychoanalyst trained in the social sciences. Chapter 2 is therefore a theoretical one that gives a theoretical framework for the rest of the book. Chapter 3, by Barbara Harris, provides the historical perspective through a lengthy and insightful analysis of women's social options for career and motherhood in the United States over the last 100 years, and particularly of the legacy of the postindustrial, Victorian cult of domesticity.

The next four chapters explore psychoanalytic insights into dual-role identity and reformulations of the psychoanalytic psychology of women, largely focusing on the concepts of self and identity. They are all by women psychoanalysts who are living a dual-role identity and who have given considerable thought to the psychological factors involved. The first is by Dr. Esther Menaker, one of the senior and most influential members of the nonmedical psychoanalytic community, who was on the original panel. She argues that the achievement of dual-role identity in women is an example of sociopsychological evolution, but that like other such evolutionary changes it can sometimes be fraught with considerable conflicts, anxieties, and guilt. She traces some of this to unconscious factors involving early identifications and counteridentifications with the mother and their later effects as women with careers have children.

The second of the psychoanalytic chapters is by Doris Bernstein, also on the original panel and currently president of the Institute of Psychoanalytic Training and Research (I.P.T.A.R.) and a faculty member there and at N.P.A.P. She endeavors to reformulate several issues in the psychoanalytic psychology of women, such as female individuation, problems of women's superego and ego ideal, and early identification processes, all of which are crucial to a later identity synthesis. She also delves into the crucial relationship of the girl with her father, and then into the psychology of men as fathers and husbands in their changing roles in the family.

Chapters 6 and 7 are by Charlotte Kahn and Harriette Podhoretz, respectively. Both are faculty members of the N.P.A.P.; Dr. Kahn is a professor of psychology at Syracuse University, and Dr. Podhoretz is also on the faculty of the New Jersey Institute for Training in Psychoanalysis. Since both women are trained in psychology as well as psychoanalysis, their chapters integrate psychological research with psychoanalytic insights. Dr. Kahn investigates psychological factors from childhood in women who were successfully carrying out a dual role of career and motherhood before the advent and support of the women's movement. Dr. Podhoretz explores some of the unconscious factors behind the "motive to avoid success" in women who are strongly oriented toward a career and who are blocked in carrying it out.

Chapter 8, which deals with the artist as mother, is by Jane Lazarre. She discusses particular problems of these women such as the periods of intense emotional involvement in artwork and its effects on the children, the double self of the artist (artistic and social), and the problems related to social recognition, particularly when little money may be earned in a culture that prizes earning capacity.

The concluding chapter, by Professor Harris and myself, historian and psychoanalyst, respectively, is an attempt to integrate the sociohistorical literature with the psychoanalytic. In other words, we present a multifaceted picture of the different dimensions and levels affecting the achievement of a dual-role identity in women and the reverberations on men.

Finally, a statement of some of the guiding principles behind the book is in order. The first is our emphasis on career. This is in no way a denigration of those women who work, but who do not consider their work particularly as a career. There is no question that many women who work in a variety of jobs gain important gratifications, such as a sense of achievement, recognition and status, and economic independence. However, we have chosen to focus on career, because it implies a certain emotional commitment and striving to realize oneself and one's potentials in the world of work, and an involvement in a type of work that often has strong, intrinsic demands. Not that career and job can always be so easily differentiated. Nor does having a career always imply the earning of significant income, as is obviously the case of many women artists.

We should probably state explicitly that this book is not meant to urge women to have both careers and children. Whatever roles and identity a particular woman wishes to work out for herself in our society is obviously very much up to her. Different roles and identities may suit a variety of temperaments and needs. We also do not assume that women who have careers and children are necessarily married. Many are separated or divorced, but there is often a man or men in their lives. Nor is this book meant to be a "how-to" manual, although some of the practical difficulties in achieving dual-role identity are discussed at length. Instead, we are concerned with a sociohistorical-psychoanalytic investigation into the variety of factors that affect women who have combined or are considering combining careers with motherhood. Thus, our orientation is toward an extensive and intensive understanding of the new identity integration involving career and motherhood; in current terminology, this is called consciousness-raising. In this case, it is for both sexes.

Our last guiding principle is to present ideas, insights, and concepts from varied disciplines in depth, but in a form readily available to the intelligent reader. We believe, for instance, that psychoanalytic understanding can be conveyed to the educated person who is untrained in psychoanalysis without sacrificing or watering down its insights. The same, of course, is true for sociohistorical factors.

Alan Roland
New York
June 1978

Chapter 1

TWO LIVES, ONE 24-HOUR DAY

Barbara Harris, Ph.D.

The conflict between professional careers and the woman's role within the family has been a persistent theme in the history of American women ever since women demanded access to the professions over a century ago. The cult of domesticity, Darwinism, doctrines of sexual liberation, and psychoanalytic theory successively defined woman's nature and capacities in such a way that for her to pursue a career was regarded as unnatural, doomed to failure, a guarantee of personal unhappiness, or all three at once. Nonetheless, since World War II, increasing numbers of females—the majority wives and mothers—have entered the labor force. Today 44.4% of all wives and 46% of all mothers with children under 18 work outside the home.[1] In most cases their motives are economic or a response to a demographic pattern in which women have fewer children and live longer.

With the rebirth of feminism in the early 1960s, there was a resurgence of social theory, dormant since the 1920s, which minimized the biological and innate differences between the sexes, demanded and advocated careers for females, and generally recommended a more androgynous life-style for both men and women. Psychoanalytic theory developed new perspectives, emphasizing ego development and self-actualization, that are much more supportive of the life-style and aspirations of the career mother.

Nonetheless, combining motherhood with a professional career is not easy for women in contemporary America. Succeeding chapters in this volume will discuss two aspects of their problems: the psychological and the historical-cultural. There is still a third dimension to be explored —the practical. Our society demands a full-time commitment from both its successful professionals and its mothers and therefore makes it exceedingly difficult for women to function in both roles. Furthermore, practical problems often trigger conflict, anxiety, and guilt that seem to derive from deep problems of identity, but that might never appear if women with children and careers found it easier to function on a day-to-day basis. In this chapter I will concentrate first on the problems of the professional woman as a mother, and then on the problems of the mother as a professional.

The primary practical problem facing a mother who has decided to pursue a career is child care. In most homes the mother assumes the responsibility for making the necessary substitute arrangements, since child care is considered her domain. Even husbands who heartily endorse their wives' careers tend to feel this way unless their wives are particularly outspoken about the joint responsibility of parenthood. In the same way, in most homes, the mother deals alone with the inconvenience that occurs when child-care arrangements fail. Only the woman who consciously resists this division of labor and is willing to spend time and energy bringing her husband around to her point of view avoids this trap.

The relatively peripheral participation of fathers in solving child-care problems is a direct result of the roles assigned to men in our society. The same set of assumptions that defines women as mothers defines men as workers and reduces fatherhood to a peripheral male role. Men are taught to value themselves in terms of their financial and professional success instead of in terms of their performance as fathers. Since professional women are likely to marry men of similar background and aspirations, the fathers of their children are often among the most career-oriented in our society. In my own case, for example, my husband is an extremely ambitious, professionally involved lawyer, who specializes in litigation. From Monday to Friday he leaves home at 8 or 9 A.M. and returns at 7 or 8 P.M. He works until 10 or 11 P.M. or attends a professional meeting once or twice a week. When he is trying a case or even preparing for trial, his hours are still longer and often spill over into weekends. Realistically, there is little question of his assuming much responsibility for child care. Unless the whole structure of his profession or his personal goals change, neither of which seems likely, his work pattern is a given in our home. Since my career ambitions have also always been accepted as a given, this does not seem unjust, but it certainly limits the possibility of solving the problem of child care in our home through shared parenting.

In my experience academic couples are the only professionals who regularly share child care on an equal basis. The crucial operative factor is that academic schedules are extremely flexible and contain relatively few fixed hours when an individual must be away from home. The academic world is also more supportive than most environments of couples who share child care. Men who express nurturant qualities and spend a great deal of time with their children are admired, not criticized for being unmasculine or unambitious. For most professional couples, however, the demands of their careers preclude this pattern of shared parenting and, given the cultural context of our society, force mothers to solve the problem of child care on their own. Professionals who are single parents, whether male or female, are in a similar situation.

What professionals who are responsible for children need are loving, competent, reliable substitutes, who are available for long, somewhat flexible hours. Until their offspring attend school a full day, they have almost no alternative to hiring a full-time mother substitute. Nothing else really frees the professional woman for total involvement in her career without depriving her children of the physical care and emotional support they need.

There are, however, two major problems with this method of taking care of one's children, one practical, the other emotional. The practical difficulty is that full-time, private child care is prohibitively expensive. In New York City at the moment, for example, a babysitter working 40 hours per week earns between $100 and $150 plus Social Security and Unemployment Insurance tax. A woman must have a relatively high income or a husband able to support the family without her help to be able to afford this expense. To put the reality in perspective, in 1974 82% of the women employed full time earned under $10,000 a year[2]; in 1973 the median income of families where both husband and wife were in the labor force was $15,237[3]. Although professional women and couples both often earn considerably more than these figures, it is clear that only a tiny percentage of families can spend $6,000 to $9,000 a year on child care.

Aside from the issue of cost, many professional women are unhappy about leaving their offspring with someone else on a regular basis. They doubt that their children will be as happy, as creatively cared for, or as culturally enriched as if they remained at home. Fundamentally they believe that children are better off if their own mothers care for them and have internalized the traditional view that successful motherhood is a full-time job. Women with professional ambitions often recognize that they do not desire to be, and are tempermentally unsuited to be, full-time mothers without completely discarding these attitudes. The result is that they return to their careers, hire a full-time babysitter, and suffer. On some level they feel selfish about their choice and experience guilt and anxiety. Anyone who has spent time around professional women can recognize the symptoms—mothers who actively miss their children while they are at work and express regret about not spending more time with them, mothers in agony because they did not share some new or "first" experience with their children, mothers who share common professional interests but rarely talk about anything but their kids and housekeepers. The contrast with the conversation of their male colleagues could not be more striking. The difference is a measure of the emotional burden borne by women who pursue careers in an unsupportive ideological and social environment. As an experiment, a friend and I once asked our respective husbands if they had ever discussed their babysitters in any connection with a colleague at work. Both men responded with a look of astonishment.

In addition to this kind of basic emotional conflict, hiring a full-time mother substitute often generates other kinds of tension because of the mother's complete dependence on her babysitter. Few men ever experience this kind of anxiety and worry, which in my view is one of the more serious day-to-day burdens of the career mother. This is something I can best illustrate from my own experience. I finished my Ph.D. and accepted a full-time teaching position for the coming year while I was pregnant with my son, who is now 10 years old. Clifford was born in January and I began working the following September. A few weeks before I started, I hired a full-time babysitter-housekeeper. She is an extraordinarily competent and loving woman and an exceptionally reliable employee. In the 9 years she has worked for me, she has never missed a day when I had classes without giving me enough advance warning to make alternate arrangements. However, she is also one of the many human beings who moves slowly and rarely gets anywhere on time. Until Clifford started nursery school, I could not leave for work until she arrived. I cannot tell you the agonies I suffered waiting for her. I was in a constant state of anxiety lest she be later than usual and I miss a class. During the first year, before I knew her well, I lived in terror that she was not simply late, but was not coming at all. Once Clifford started school and my husband or I dropped him off in the morning and then continued on to work, I felt as if an enormous weight had been lifted from my shoulders.

The alternative to private child care of the kind I have been describing is some sort of collective child-care arrangement. Indeed, given the economics of the situation, most American mothers will be free to pursue careers only when high-quality, low-cost day-care centers are available to every parent who needs them. Such a system requires massive financial support from the federal government, support that will not be forthcoming until our society has undergone a major transformation in its attitudes toward both women and children. Feminists are correct in their insistence that day care is a key issue on which no compromise is ultimately possible. Without adequate facilities for all mothers, only a small, elite group of women will be able to pursue their professional or artistic careers as wholeheartedly and successfully as their male peers.

Unfortunately, despite their financial advantages, most professional women are even more reluctant to use day-care centers than they are to hire full-time babysitters[4]. Even if they accept that children can flourish in the care of mother substitutes, they put a great deal of emphasis on a "one-to-one" relationship between the infant or young child and mothering person. This is true in spite of the fact that most first children share their mothers with a sibling after a few years and that subsequent children never have them all to themselves. The ambivalence of professional women about communal forms of child rearing is, I think, one of the reasons that feminists have been so unsuccessful in securing governmental support for them. On a political level, too, day-care centers are still often seen as destructive of the American family, damaging to children, and an insidious way of extending governmental influence into the home. Furthermore, since the day-care controversy has become connected to the issue of welfare reform, the whole concept has become associated with low-cost, compulsory care for the offspring of the poor, a development that has not endeared the idea to the professional classes. Jane Lazarre's *The Mother Knot* contains a moving rebuttal of this whole point of view and demonstrates both the importance of day-care centers for mothers with careers but little income and the happiness of children lucky enough to attend good ones.

Once children attend school a full day the problem of caring for them becomes much simpler. Whatever our schools teach or do not teach the young, they function relatively efficiently as child-care institutions, although they do not totally fill the needs of professional mothers. Children still need to be supervised after school and during vacations and must be taken care of when they are ill. The mother's hours at work, the child's age, the availability of grandparents and neighbors, the family's financial resources, and the parents' attitude toward leaving their offspring unsupervised all influence the way a particular career mother handles these situations. However, she invariably has more options than when her child was very young. Schools often run a whole range of athletic, art, music, and drama programs after regular hours. Many cities have private or service organizations that do likewise, some for a fee and some without cost. A part-time babysitter, even a teenager in the neighborhood, can often cover the hours before one of the child's parents returns from work. In the summer, school-age children can attend a whole variety of day or sleep-away camps.

The usefulness of schools as child-care institutions is a major reason for the appeal of private nursery schools to the educated, middle-class women who can afford them[5]. Nursery schools are considered good for young children and therefore allow mothers to pursue their careers without feeling guilty. Pressure from women who use them instead of other forms of child care is one of the reasons that more and more nursery schools are running all day programs for 4- and 5-year-olds.

This perspective on the function of schools raises a serious question about the sanctity of the long summer vacation. It developed originally because schoolchildren, predominately boys, were needed on the farm during the busy summer months. In a highly industrialized, urbanized economy this rationale no longer exists, and serious consideration should be given to running schools 11 or 12 months a year, with an option for a longer vacation in families where it is convenient. It would immeasurably simplify the lives of professional women, especially those who cannot afford summer camp. Furthermore, if the educational system recognized and accepted this function, it might be easier to extend the notion that society has a responsibility for child care to those below school age.

Because they already feel guilty and anxious, mothers with careers are particularly ill-equipped to handle minor crises in their children's lives. Whether or not their mothers work, almost all babies and young children go through periods when they express distress at their mother's departure. It is the rare woman who can close the door on her screaming baby morning after morning without wondering whether she is not doing untold, irreparable emotional damage to her child. I remember well the period in my son's life—sometime in his second year—when he lay down in front of the door and started crying, "Don't leave, don't leave," every time I put my coat on to go to work. Not for me the cheerful "by-by" that accompanied his father out the door each morning. What enabled me to step over his prone body, voice a cheerful, "Have a nice day and be a good boy," and turn my thoughts to the class I was about to teach was a story my own mother, also a career woman, once told me. She said that at some point before I started nursery school, I began to throw tantrums every morning as she left for work. She asked our babysitter if anything had happened to make me particularly unhappy. Mame's response was to suggest that the next morning my mother slam the front door as if she were leaving but remain on the inside. My mother followed these directions and discovered that the minute the door slammed the agonized screams from the rear of the house stopped. To her astonishment she heard me say, "Mommy's gone now, Mame. It's time to play." With this story to help me put my own son's behavior in perspective and to remind me not to take the desire of children to possess and control their mothers too seriously, I was able to live through this period without undue emotional wear and tear.

Whenever their children go through difficult periods or misbehave in particularly dramatic ways, mothers with careers tend to blame themselves and to question whether they were right, after all, to pursue their professions. At such times they forget all the ill-behaved and disturbed children they know whose mothers stay at home. Once when my son was in first grade, he threw a tantrum of major proportions when my housekeeper picked him up at school. My babysitter was totally humiliated both by his conduct and her inability to control him. Furious that I had been publicly disgraced and needing to placate my housekeeper, who was threatening to quit unless "I did something about Clifford," I meted out a draconic but well-deserved punishment. As soon as I was left alone, however, my anger melted away and I was overwhelmed by a sense of complete failure. I felt completely responsible for my son's behavior and kept asking myself what I had done to create such a monster. For the first time I wondered aloud whether I had damaged my son irreparably by neglecting him in order to pursue my career. Calls from a number of women in the neighborhood who had witnessed the scene only made matters worse. They all wanted me to know exactly what happened and suggested in one way or another that such things would not occur if I spent more time at home. Although I responded bravely that this was impossible and Clifford would simply have to adjust to the mother he had, I no longer believed a word I was saying and felt my longstanding convictions about the emptiness of full-time motherhood evaporating into thin air. Depressed, humiliated, and guilt-ridden, I took to my bed, wondering how I would ever summon the courage to leave it and walk down Montague Street again.

When my husband arrived a few hours later, he entered a silent, dark apartment. Clifford was confined to his room under the strictest orders not to leave it on penalty of death. I was in bed with the lights out and my head under the pillow. When I explained what had happened, Joel's eyes opened wider than usual, and he looked at me as if I were totally crazy. I do not remember everything he said, but the gist of it was that Clifford Harris was old enough to assume responsiblity for his own behavior. If he chose to act like a monster, that was his problem, not mine, and he was the one who would suffer. In any case, all the kids he knew were barbarians, whether their mothers worked or not. As for me, he had never seen a worse example of a would-be feminist in his life. The first time a bunch of malicious women, probably jealous of my career, insinuated that Clifford's terrible behavior was my fault, I went completely to pieces. Why did I suddenly think that children were their mothers' puppets? Didn't he, Joel Harris, count in his son's life at all? And, finally, what had happened to my vision of the child as an autonomous, self-motivated individual? By the time Joel finished, I was beginning to regain my equilibrium. Although it was a few weeks before I stopped wondering what various women in the neighborhood thought about me and my horrid child, my husband's sincere and firm enunciation of my customary views restored my faith in them and in the life-style I had chosen.[6]

This incident is a perfect example of how important feedback from other people is in facilitating or undermining the efforts of women to combine their careers with motherhood. In a society still influenced by the legacy of the cult of domesticity, such women are bound to feel insecure and responsible when faced by the normal problems and misbehavior of childhood. At such times mothers in traditional roles all too often seize the opportunity to in-

crease the career mother's anxiety. This happens so frequently that it is hard to avoid the conclusion that mothers
with careers frequently arouse the jealousy and/or hostility
of more traditional women. Some mothers who stay at
home act as if the career mother's attempt to combine two
roles is a standing reproach to women who have not made
the effort.[7] On the occasion recounted above, I felt very
strongly that a number of the women who called me about
it were fundamentally pleased that Clifford had behaved so
badly. Usually I toss off remarks indicating disapproval of
my life-style and give them little thought, but I will never
forget the one occasion when I felt completely vulnerable.

Women combining motherhood and careers are not,
of course, completely bereft of emotional support. Their
husbands often play a crucial role in facilitating their dual
roles. This is certainly true in my case. Indeed, I have often
felt that my relative lack of conflict about combining a career with motherhood is due largely to Joel's genuine pref-
erence for women with professions, his pleasure and pride
in my success, and his sincere conviction that Clifford is
better off because his mother has a career. Sociological
studies of professional mothers reveal that many men feel
this way about their wives' careers.[8]

Mothers with professions also receive encouragement
and support from other women—not the traditional
women who resent their life-styles, but those who share
their aspirations and understand their problems and conflicts. I have found the women I work with and those I have
met in professional and feminist organizations an invaluable source of strength, empathy, and practical advice. As
more and more women combine their roles as professionals and mothers, these networks of support will grow
stronger and more extensive, greatly reducing the impact
of an hostile social environment.

Finally, as more and more women with careers successfully raise their children, women will find it easier to define

motherhood as a part-time job and to rely on private or collective mother substitutes. Nontraditional patterns of child care will be increasingly common and therefore more acceptable. Perhaps most important, the daughters of these women will grow up with a new set of identifications that enables them to see combining motherhood and a career as desirable and natural. In my own case, for example, it was easier for me to combine motherhood and a career because my own mother did so throughout my childhood. As a number of essays in this volume will show, primary identifications with the mother are crucial in the creation of the adult female identity. In the long run, therefore, the development of a new, socially acceptable identity—that of the career mother—may well grow naturally out of current employment trends.

Thus far I have been discussing the problems of the professional woman as a mother. Now I would like to discuss the problems of the mother as a professional. Here the key issue is time. Successful professional and artistic careers often require almost unlimited amounts of time and energy, at least at certain periods. Yet unlimited time and energy are precisely what the career mother does not have. By definition she has chosen to compartmentalize her life and divide her time. In very structured professions this often means that she cannot compete with men who assume far fewer family responsibilities, and she advances much more slowly than men do. Women who have internalized the standards of their field and set high goals for themselves suffer a great deal over their slower progress. Although they understand the reasons for it intellectually, they often begin to doubt their own abilities. In my profession, college teaching, for example, I know many women with children who have held full-time positions from the time their offspring were babies. One of their most typical complaints is that they have not published as much as they expected to when they were graduate students. In many cases they have begun to doubt whether they ever will publish a book—even though they consider this a minimal requirement for satisfactory performance in their fields. With these lower levels of publication go denied promotions and rejected applications for fellowships—all of which further damage their self-esteem.

In my husband's profession, the law, success in the large prestigious firms requires putting a commitment to one's work before anything else. A willingness to work long hours in the evening and on weekends is expected of everyone. Women with children who cannot and will not (rightfully) work these hours simply cannot succeed in this world, which certainly represents the highest echelons of the legal profession. To give another example from the law, litigation in any form is a difficult specialty for the career mother because the demands on the time and energy of the attorney preparing and trying a case are almost unlimited. During a trial, the litigator is usually so involved in it that he or she is both unable and unwilling to think about much else. If the litigator is a mother, who will take care of the kids in the meantime?

The solution to the professional problems of women with children is not to penalize them for assuming one of society's most important roles or to encourage them to forego the very real joys and satisfactions of mothering, but to restructure the professions to meet their needs and life cycles. Men as well as women would benefit from the result; although the professions developed in ways that ostensibly reflect and fill the needs of men, in practice they require men to sacrifice their personal and emotional lives to their desire for material success and prestige. In any case, equal opportunity for women can never exist until fundamental change of this sort occurs. Without it, even the most conscientious, universal enforcement of affirmative action plans will not succeed in bringing large numbers of women into the upper levels of their professions. In academia, for example, most universities and colleges require a faculty member to publish a book before granting tenure, a decision normally taken 6 years after the person is hired. These are the very years when women with Ph.D.'s are most likely to have infants and young children and to find it most difficut to do research and publish. The result is that they are less successful than men with similar educational backgrounds in finding permanent positions and end up in disproportionate numbers in less prestigious institutions. To accommodate the career mother, academia either has to waive the requirement of a published book or postpone the tenure decision. Although this sort of suggestion is bound to raise the cry of undermining professional standards, nothing short of this kind of reform in every profession will permit mothers to function equally in their careers.

Until that far-off day, mothers in the professions will continue to struggle to fill two full-time roles at once, an effort that inevitably prevents them from meeting either set of their obligations to their complete satisfaction. The constant pressure that they are under accounts for one of the traits most characteristic of the daily lives of career mothers —their obsession with time. Only women who schedule their day carefully, work efficiently, move quickly, and go to bed late can even attempt to combine the maternal and professional roles. No wonder that at a recent meeting of woman historians I looked around the room and noticed that virtually everyone looked exhausted!

Many women partially solve the problem of budgeting their time by defining almost everything besides their activities as professionals and mothers as of secondary importance. They often reevaluate their conception of the wife's role and alter their behavior accordingly. The effect of this kind of adjustment on their marriages depends as much on their husband's attitudes as their own. A man who identifies with his mate's professional success and attaches great importance to it will willingly surrender some of the traditional services of the wife, while a man who resents or is indifferent to his wife's career will not.

The kind of adjustment I am talking about may involve increased sharing of domestic chores, a one-sided or joint decision to give up certain activities considered important in most homes and in most marriages, or a conscious and careful compartmentalization of the joint activities of the couple to suit their respective professional schedules. The necessity of carefully planning schedules to accommodate the wife's dual role invariably deprives the family of flexibility and spontaneity in its daily life. Couples in such homes find it difficult to go out to dinner or to the movies at the last moment. When the husband unexpectedly finds himself with a free evening because a meeting was cancelled, his wife is invariably snowed under with work, or vice versa. They can rarely accompany each other on business trips, no matter how tempting. In the last 2 years, for example, I have had to forego three trips to Mexico and one to Japan.

In our home, my husband and I spend very little time together from Monday to Friday, except for a rather hurried breakfast and an hour or so late in the evening. My housekeeper usually gives dinner to my son, who is ready to eat hours before Joel or I come home. When either of us is there at dinner time, he or she puts together an *ad hoc* meal from things in the refrigerator or freezer or brings in Chinese food. This kind of arrangement suits both our working patterns. Joel needs to be flexible about when he leaves his office and hates being tied down to a fixed dinner hour, while I want both a flexible schedule and freedom from responsibility for planning and cooking meals. Although we are both involved in evening professional activities, we make a conscious effort to keep the nights when we are both out to a minimum. We do try to save one evening a week for going out alone together.

Generally we spend weekends at our home in the Berkshires. We share household chores such as marketing and cooking and spend a lot of time in activities our son enjoys. When we go out, we usually take him with us. We often invite friends for the weekend, entertaining informally so that Clifford and any children they bring fit in easily. We enjoy the "togetherness" of our weekends because it contrasts so sharply with our everyday patterns.

The arrangement of our life is one example of the way in which two people have tried to accommodate dual commitments to their family and professions. Each couple has, of course, to work out its own pattern. One of the few generalizations that can be made about this process is that in apportioning their time, professional women are more likely to reject some of the wife's traditional functions than to neglect their roles as mothers. In other words, their husbands are more likely to suffer from their tight schedules than their children.[9] Therefore, the potential for marital conflict traceable to the wife's career is often high, particularly if the husband has fairly set ideas about women's roles. The question of who is going to plan, prepare, and clean up from dinner may well develop into a major battleground. Joel and I have solved this problem by eliminating the joint evening meal from Monday to Friday. More often couples share these functions or the woman continues to perform them in return for help in some other area of the home. Sometimes traditional arrangements are so important to the husband that the wife carries on alone, no matter how tired or resentful she feels.

Conflict may also grow out of the common assumption that running the household is the wife's responsibility. Professional couples often hire someone to take over as many domestic functions as possible. Other couples share essential chores and virtually ignore all the others. Many professional women consciously reject the standards of cleanliness and order advocated by instruments of popular culture such as women's magazines and T.V. Their casual attitude toward housekeeping reflects a healthy reordering of priorities.

When their wives raise the issue, many men agree readily to share household tasks. As Pat Mainardi points out in her marvelous essay, "The Politics of Housework," the wife's problem has only begun when her husband promises to take over certain chores.[10] The real challenge is to get him to do them regularly so that she no longer has to think about them at all. This often requires a good deal of tact and persistance on her part as well as a willingness to accept that her husband may not do the job as well as she thinks he ought to. This is something I learned a number of years ago myself when Joel and I divided responsibility for cleaning our country house. I agreed to do the kitchen, Clifford the two bathrooms, and Joel the rest of the house. The result was that Joel never vacuumed when I thought it was necessary unless I reminded, even nagged, him. I hated the position this put me in and finally decided (perhaps after reading Mainardi's essay) that I was not going to remind him again, no matter how dirty the house got, nor was I going to do the job myself. Weeks went by and the dust under couches, chairs, and tables got thicker and thicker. When people came over, I felt terribly embarrassed about the state of the living room. After all, no one blames a husband for a dirty house. Still, I said and did nothing. Finally, when I had almost given up hope, Joel remarked that the house was filthy. I replied that I knew and had been wondering when he was going to vacuum. For a minute he got a blank look on his face, then he said, "Oh, yeah, I'm supposed to do that, aren't I?" I wish I could report that from then on, Joel was a reformed man, but I cannot. He still lets the house get far dustier than I would like, but sooner or later does notice and do the job. What I learned from the experience is that the wife cannot have it both ways—either she does the job herself or she accepts the way her husband does it and truly frees herself from responsibility.

In addition to the obvious area of housework, tension may develop between the professional woman and her husband because her time is not at his disposal. Men with traditional expectations assume that their wives will be home when they return from work to cater to their needs and to share leisure activities. They expect their wives to entertain their friends and, in general, to take care of their common social life. They often also expect their wives to entertain and socialize with their business or professional associates and clients. In many occupations, particularly those connected to large corporations, wives are openly recognized as assets or detriments to their husbands' careers.

Many women with children and professions of their own are even more hostile to traditional expectations in this area than in the area of housework. They particularly resent being asked to spend time advancing their husband's careers at the expense of their own. Fortunately, neither Joel nor I is in a professional position where much socializing or entertaining as a couple is necessary. On the infrequent occasions when it is, we try to accommodate each other, always recognizing that the other's own professional obligations come first. Actually, I go out with Joel's business associates and clients so rarely that I rather enjoy it and occasionally ask if I can come along when he is taking someone out to dinner. In our personal lives both of us would like to entertain and go out more. At the moment we cannot manage it and have accepted that things probably will not change much until Clifford grows up.

In some respects I found it harder than Joel to put my career first. To my surprise, some of my automatic responses as a wife and mother were extremely conventional. For example, I used to feel mildly guilty every time I returned from a meeting and found Joel at home. On some level I obviously thought that I ought to be there when he was. Interestingly, Joel never felt that way, and over the years I have gotten over that reaction. Similarly, I experienced guilt and anxiety the first few times I went to professional meetings away from home. My internal conflict expressed itself in giving both my husband and housekeeper elaborate (and mostly unnecessary) instructions about what to do in every possible contingency. Joel got very annoyed at being treated like a total incompetent, and when I returned always told me pointedly how well he and Clifford had managed. The problem was obviously mine, not his. I felt torn between my obligations as a wife and mother and as a professional, a conflict that is almost inevitable in a society that defines the domestic and professional roles as ours does. Perhaps what the woman with a child and a career needs to learn first is to accept and live with the tension and anxiety built into her life.

What I hope I have made clear is that it is much more difficult than it need be for mothers with a career to evolve a satisfactory life-style. Restructuring the professions and creating a comprehensive system of superior day-care centers would immeasurably simplify their practical problems. A transformation in consciousness that eliminates the legacy of the cult of domesticity would make these changes possible and eliminate much of the external and internal conflict career mothers experience. The ideological significance of biological determinism, which influences both revisionist psychoanalytic theory and the latest intellectual fad, "biosociology," must be recognized, so that it is deprived of its appeal as "objective" science. As I will show in Chapter 3, economic and social forces in the late eighteenth and nineteenth centuries restricted women to the home and excluded them from the evolving professions; biological determinism in various forms functioned as the intellectual justification of that process. The definition of

women as mothers and of motherhood as a full-time occupation is anachronistic in a country where nearly half the
children under 18 have working mothers[11] and both the
husband and wife work in almost half the marriages. A
more appropriate definition of womanhood and more supportive social institutions are needed to encourage and
enable more women to experience the great joy that comes
from combining motherhood with professional success.

Chapter 2

IDENTITY AS AN ORIENTING CONCEPT

Alan Roland, Ph.D.

It is no accident that the psychoanalytic concept of identity evolved in only the last 25 years or so, and in the United States at that. It is also significant that Freud mentioned identity only once, and in a nonprofessional paper.[1] In all the multiplicity of directions he explored, it is clear that identity was not one of them.

Why is it, then, that this concept, so new in the psychoanalytic field, has paradoxically so captured the modern imagination? And why is it that identity, at least identity conflicts and syntheses as developed by Erikson,[2] is one of the only psychoanalytic concepts not directly concerned with early childhood experiences but, instead, pertains to late adolescence and early adulthood? The answers, I am sure, must involve historical and social change and the nature of psychoanalysis.

Psychoanalysis is the study of anomalous phenomena (i.e., insight and understanding of the unconscious are brought to bear when things go amiss in the individual). In late nineteenth-century Vienna, Freud's attention was first drawn to hysteria and repressed sexuality. These were not the only psychological problems of his time, nor did his hysterical patients suffer only from repression of sexuality, as is now evident from a reworking of his case material. But in the Victorian era in which he lived, where sexuality in middle-class women was so repressed, these problems cried out for understanding and solution.

In contemporary American society, problems created by sexual repression are no longer so central a concern. Instead, emotional difficulties around the development of the self and its incorporation into a later ego synthesis of identity have emerged as focal points for psychoanalytic investigation and therapy. Many women and men experience considerable difficulties in arriving at such an inner synthesis, and they are more beset by identity conflicts than resolutions. Or, in many educated women, it has often taken the form of an adult identity synthesis that precludes the inclusion of many of the potentialities and abilities developed during childhood and adolescence. This is not even to speak of the often tumultuous adolescent identity crises that Erikson so insightfully described. Thus, identity has come under psychological scrutiny in a way it has never been before.

But what is an "identity synthesis"? It is usually a late adolescent and early adulthood psychological achievement, encompassing an inner psychological integration—partly conscious and partly unconscious—of childhood and adolescent psychological elements with the choosing of and commitment to a value system (ideology in Erikson's terms) and to various important adult roles involving work, love, and social relationships. A sense of inner continuity with the past and an inner synthesis that reaches into the future develop.

For instance, when women strive to have both careers and children, it is not simply that they are trying to combine different social roles. A rearrangement of the inner furniture of the mind and emotional life must occur. Psychological elements pertaining to the roles of mother and of career must not only be worked out but, equally important, some relative inner harmony between varying emotional elements related to *both* of these roles must develop. Thus, successfully combining career and motherhood implies an inner psychological achievement as well as an achievement in social reality; the concept of identity explicitly and implicitly encompasses both.

In working out such an inner synthesis, an individual does not necessarily have to adjust to a given society or be limited to the various options that a society presents to its members. There is certainly room in the integration of identity for innovative efforts to fashion roles and values at variance with or a step beyond those predominant in a given era, or to effect change in the social structure. Today, women working out careers and family are a case in point.

In American society, this dual-role identity is new enough so that many of these women are fashioning very new role patterns, value systems and ideals, and kinds of relationships; they are setting significant patterns that will be far easier for other women to follow in the future. And yet it must be emphasized that it is rare for an individual to depart very far from the existing opportunities within a given society without significant support from some others. Only the extremely rare person can forego support, recognition, and confirmation of their particular identity.

But why has it become so difficult to achieve an adult identity today? Generally, it is probably due to the enormous social mobility that at least the middle class has, and to the tremendous loosening up, if not at times partial disintegration, of traditional roles and values in American society. Thus, it is mainly in modern times that individuals are completely free to choose a mate (or not) and to choose their own occupation. Traditional family roles in much of contemporary American society no longer exert the influence they once did. And the existence of a value system or ideology validated by social consensus is almost gone. On the one hand, the opportunities for individual choice and autonomy are immeasurably greater today than ever before. Even innovations in roles and life-styles may be easier to accomplish today than in earlier eras. As Chapter 3 demonstrates, in the United States it is only in the present era that it is reasonably possible for women to have careers and children. On the other hand, the strains on the individual are also immeasurably greater, because there are far fewer social guidelines and supports for adult roles and values than in previous historical eras.

Therefore, the study of identity conflicts and syntheses has been brought about by significant social change. It has enabled the psychoanalyst to consider the other main dimension of identity—the conscious and unconscious psychological elements of childhood and adolescence. Of what do these consist? Certainly one crucial element is childhood identifications. In infancy, these first take place with the mother or mothering person, who sometimes can be a grandmother, aunt, maid, or, more often today, the father, and then a little later with the mother and father. These early childhood identifications occur more unconsciously; in later childhood and adolescence, identifications occur through more conscious, selective choice of esteemed traits of the adult or even older children. A crucial part of this identification process is the consolidation of the child's sex role (i.e., her or his identification with the parent of the same sex). This, as well as other identifications, is central to the formation of personality and functioning in the world. A variation of this process is counteridentifications, where the child explicitly rejects the parent he or she has and forms identifications with other adults who are different. But underlying these conscious counteridentifications are usually unconscious identifications. Or there may be forbidden identifications, where one parent forbids the child to identify with the other parent and the child complies out of loyalty.

Another important part of the identification process is the emulation of certain role models. The ego-ideal derives partly from certain idealizations of the parents and other figures and partly from incorporating certain parental expectations. These expectations may be conscious or unconscious on the parent's part; they often are gradually incorporated by children from infancy on and form crucial identity themes around which persons may unconsciously orient their life. Then there is the development of the superego or the unconscious conscience of the child—the incorporation of the do's and don'ts, of what a child is permitted or not permitted to be. For instance, it becomes important how assertive and competitive a girl is allowed to be compared to a boy.

Still another crucial element in the formation of identity is the child's need for close emotional attachment to the mother as well as the need to separate and individuate from her. The mothering person's attitudes and ways of relating to these needs of her child are also internalized. What variations of automony as well as of closeness are permitted to each child are crucial elements in personality formation. The relationship of the child with the father is also important. Although psychoanalysis has focused more on the relationship with the mothering person in very recent years, as the result mainly of the work of women psychoanalysts such as Anna Freud, Melanie Klein, Margaret Mahler, and Edith Jacobson,[3] this contrasts with Freud's emphasis on the father. The relationship with the father is a crucial identity element for the girl as well as the boy and will be discussed at some length in Chapter 5.

Another important identity element is the self-image derived from the mirroring relationship with the mothering person of very early childhood. That is, the mothering person reflects back to the infant and young child how important or valued he or she is. Young children read in the other's face what they are like, how much they are liked, and how they exist in the Other's mind. The basic self-image and sense of self-worth largely derive from this early mirroring relationship with the mothering person.

Finally, there are crucial identity elements from adolescence, including various identifications with the peer group, which assume an increasingly greater weight in contemporary American culture as the influence of the family wanes. In more traditional family structures, the father's attitudes for both son and daughter about work are usually internalized as an important identity element of how the adolescent will relate to the work world. In any case, all of the elements mentioned go into the integration of an adult identity, but not in a linear, one-to-one relationship. As Erikson emphasizes, an identity synthesis includes but also transcends earlier identifications, and this would also be true of self-image, ego-ideal, superego, and identity themes. The whole is greater than the sum of its parts, and what may have been a fairly major note in childhood, or even in adolescence, may be played softly in a later identity synthesis. Or, in the case of many women, important earlier identity elements may be quite precluded in a later adult identity involving traditional roles. Bernstein[4] cites some evidence of a childhood identity synthesis where sex-role identifications of the oedipal period (around age 6 years) are synthesized with earlier identifications, self-image, and so on. But such a childhood identity synthesis would differ from a later one because involvements in adult roles and value systems are missing.

What happens in an era of rapid social change, where the identifications, and even the ego-ideals and superego, belong to models of a more traditional society? It becomes obvious that such a situation, which exists today, is filled with the potential for inner conflict, as well as new resolutions. As will be discussed in Chapter 4, we may have situations where there are deep, childhood identifications with a traditional housewife-mother on a woman's part; however, conscious values exist that transcend such a role model. Or, in other situations, a father may respect and encourage a daughter's achievement, but denigrate women in more traditional mothering roles. It is obvious that in different ways, each of these situations will introduce conflict in any later identity synthesis that seeks to integrate career and motherhood.

A final but crucial aspect to any identity synthesis is that no one lives in a vacuum. Any adult needs some amount of continuous mirroring or affirmation in love, work, and social relationships about the kind of person, identity, and style of life she or he is trying to work out and be. This becomes particularly important in evolving any new identity, except for those rare, highly resolute individuals who feed off of some inner source of strength. There is no question that women who are trying to work out a dual-role identity of career and motherhood usually need confirmation from both ends of the social equation, from those at work and those at home, and also from other women who are struggling to achieve the same goal. As more role models of women doing both gradually develop, as men respond more positively and with less threat to their own identity, as this life-style becomes more entrenched in the social process, and as some of the practical arrangements become better worked out, the achievement of career and motherhood should become easier and less filled with conflict.

Chapter 3

CAREERS, CONFLICT, AND CHILDREN: THE LEGACY OF THE CULT OF DOMESTICITY

Barbara Harris, Ph.D.

Career women in late twentieth-century America experience enormous amounts of guilt and anxiety about trying to function simultaneously as wives, mothers, and professionals. Their conversations are filled with doubts about their competence as mothers and the level of their commitment to their careers. Most of all they complain about not having enough time—time to spend with their children and husbands, time to keep their households from slipping into chaos, and, above all, time to meet their expectations of themselves as professionals. The source of these conflicts is a powerful set of cultural values and social norms that tell professional women that the role of wife and mother is a full-time occupation and that it is impossible or irresponsible to try to combine it with a career. To the degree that they accept or are influenced by these attitudes, professional women are bound to feel conflict if they are also wives and mothers.

In the United States these cultural values and social norms originated in the nineteenth-century cult of domesticity or the cult of true womanhood.[1] The cult of domesticity was an ideology that prescribed behavioral models for Victorian women and was the most influential source of attitudes toward females in the period. It consisted of four basic ideas: a rigid dichotomy between the home and the economic world outside it; the belief that the home was the female's *only* proper sphere; the idea that woman is morally superior to man and the appropriate repository of ethical and cultural values; and an idealization of the female's role as mother. Although the cult of true womanhood was phrased in universal terms, it actually applied only to white, middle-class women in more settled areas of the country. The life-style it assumed and recommended took no account of the problems and harsh necessities of poor women, frontier women, and slave women. Indeed, one could argue that a privileged group of middle-class women were able to translate the cult of domesticity into reality because less fortunate females existed to be exploited sexually and as domestic servants.

At the heart of the cult of true womanhood was a rigid contrast between the home and the economic world outside it. The home was a self-contained haven set down in the brutal competitive world of early American capitalism. Presided over by a woman, "the angel of the hearth," the home preserved and transmitted religious and moral values that could not survive outside it. The lady of the house created a refuge of peace and order to which her husband could retreat after struggling to earn security and comfort for his family. Above all, she maintained domestic purity to make her home a fit place to raise virtuous Christian children. Harriot Hunt expressed a common nineteenth-century belief when she wrote, "Home is the mould of character. If it has cracks and flaws, expect to see the consequences in your children."[2] The woman sheltered her young as much as possible from the materialism, cruelty, and vice of the economic environment where men fought for success. Family bible reading, prayers, and church attendance all reflected the essentially religious character of the Victorian home.

Although nineteenth-century Americans believed that the contrast they made between the domestic and economic spheres was a traditional one, in reality their concept of society was relatively new. The colonial economy was characterized by small-scale agriculture, trade, and industry, where the home and place of business were most often the same. Wives worked alongside their husbands, contributing in essential ways to household management and family income. Men taught their daughters and wives their skills, and widows frequently carried on their mates' enterprises successfully. Women also founded and headed their own business. Julia Spruill and Elisabeth Dexter show females employed in every branch of the colonial economy. Throughout the period, single women, wives, and widows succeeded as independent entrepreneurs in a wide variety of crafts and trades.[3]

The character of the preindustrial economy thus encouraged colonists to translate the Protestant ideal of the wife as helpmate and partner into economic reality. Nonetheless, historians should not idealize the colonial period as a golden age for male-female relations.[4] However essential and efficient, women were very junior partners in the domestic economy as long as their fathers or husbands were alive. Furthermore, within family businesses, well-defined sex roles existed. Most important, the economy was not the only factor affecting the position of and attitudes toward colonial women. Religious and historical traditions that asserted the inferiority of females and prescribed their subjection to men survived and powerfully influenced law, education, and other crucial areas of society.

In the late eighteenth century the colonial economic pattern began to change. In cities along the eastern seaboard and on Southern plantations, rising standards of living encouraged women to conform to the model of the idle lady instead of to the model of the Protestant helpmate. A yearning to conform to English standards of gentility discouraged middle-class and well-to-do females from participating actively in trade. According to Spruill, fewer Southern women started their own businesses in the eighteenth than in the seventeenth century.[5] Dexter observes that there was much more criticism of middle-class women who worked outside the home after the American Revolution than before.[6] The beginning of industrialization accelerated this process in the early nineteenth century.[7] Middle-class females did not follow the textile industry out of the home. The new factory labor force came almost exclusively from the families of small farmers so that increasingly the experience of American women varied from one class to another.

In a society that put a premium on profit-making, the transformation of middle-class women from producers into consumers inevitably deprived them of status and self-esteem. The negative implications of industrialization for women were underscored by the fact that in the same period the professionalization of medicine, the development of public education, and the growth of organized philanthropy removed other traditional female functions from the home. As long as middle-class women could not follow men into the public sphere, they really did have fewer things to do that they and their culture valued. Sarah Orne Jewett expressed their sense of loss in her short story, "The Courting of Sister Wisby."[8] The political reforms of the Jacksonian era only exacerbated the situation. Native, white, middle-class women who were denied the vote felt humiliated and outraged when immigrant men, whom they considered their social and intellectual inferiors, were allowed to go to the polls.

The appeal and strength of the cult of domesticity was that it assigned middle-class women new religious and moral duties at the very time they were experiencing a significant loss of function and status, and compensated them for the loss by emphasizing their importance as wives and mothers. The cult of true womanhood reflected the emerging social reality by drawing sharper distinctions between female and male functions than previously existed in American culture, and legitimized the dichotomy by idealizing women as "angels of the hearth."

Inevitably, the influence and relevance of the cult of domesticity varied considerably from class to class and region to region. Economic necessity prevented working-class and poor women from conforming to its prescriptions, however appealing they found them. In the West, the progressive opening of the frontier preserved material and social conditions reminiscent of the colonial period long after they had disappeared in more settled parts of the country. Even in the East, women in sparsely populated, remote areas had different functions from females who lived in or near large towns or on more accessible farms. Finally, in the antebellum South, conditions shaping the lives of black women, whether slave or free, made the cult of domesticity irrelevant. Thus, class, region, and race influenced the impact of the cult of true womanhood on American females, although in general its importance as a behavioral model grew steadily in the period from 1800 to the outbreak of the Civil War.

Women's roles as domestic guardians of religious and ethical values depended on the Victorian conviction that they were more virtuous than men. Propagators of the cult of true womanhood, who traced most sin to lust, thought that women felt little, if any, sexual desire and traced their superiority to this fact. They believed that men, on the other hand, fell prey to almost uncontrollable passion. Consequently, males took the initiative in sexual relations, while women remained passive and experienced little pleasure. Wives submitted to their husbands because it was their duty to do so and to bear children.

Nineteenth-century Americans expressed persistent fears that even the best of men would fall into sexual immorality. This belief shaped their view of prostitutes. Throughout the century moral reformers regarded them as the victims of male lust instead of as inherently evil.[9] When faced with a young girl seduced by her employer, Harriot Hunt exclaimed, for example, "I had seen the unfortunate of my own sex—diseased, bloated, loathsome—allured to sin by man, and he accepted in society with fine broadcloth and kid gloves. But here before my eyes was innocence in the hour of its betrayal—beauty departed—intelligence dying out—and frankness destroyed by deception and compromise!"[10] Female moral reformers thought the cure for vice was to raise men to women's higher morality *and* to provide women with enough economic opportunities so that poverty would not drive them into vice.[11] An enormous amount of literature denounced the double standard and advocated "purity"—the confinement of sex to marriage—for both women and men. Despite this propaganda, in the event of any wrongdoing, the full force of social disapproval fell on females. Any middle-class women guilty of sexual impropriety was cast out of respectable society.

In a recent article Carl Degler challenged this interpretation of nineteenth-century attitudes toward female sexuality.[12] He denied that doctors and other experts uniformly assumed that women experienced little sexual desire or pleasure and that middle-class behavior conformed to such preconceptions. Degler certainly proved that some doctors and women recognized and accepted female sexuality in the last third of the century (his earliest source dated from 1869) and that all nineteenth-century Americans did not subscribe to the doctrines about women's sexual nature expounded by the cult of domesticity. He has not, however, solved the problem of deciding how much relative importance to attach to ideas that recognized female passion. In fact, the attitudes associated with the cult of true womanhood represented the beliefs of many more middle-class Victorian Americans than the ideas on which Degler focused.[13]

In support of his contention that nineteenth-century women both desired and enjoyed sexual relations, Degler cited a survey of the sexual behavior and attitudes of 45 women carried out by Dr. Clelia Mosher (1863–1940) of Stanford University between the early 1890s and 1920. Of the questionnaires that could be dated, 17 were completed before 1900, 14 between 1913 and 1917, and five in 1920. Of the respondents, 33 were born before 1870. For all its interest, the Mosher survey cannot sustain Degler's thesis. The size of the sample was far too small to support any generalization about middle-class women in Victorian America. Even more important, the respondents were atypical members of their class because they were far better educated. Their educations may well have influenced their attitudes toward sex. Finally, answers given to a survey conducted between 1892 and 1920 cannot be construed to be representative of nineteenth-century opinion, even if most of the respondents were born before 1870. During the thirty-year period when the survey was carried out, a revolution in attitudes toward sexuality occurred under the influence of such people as Havelock Ellis, Ellen Key, and Edward Carpenter. James McGovern dated the first sexual revolution from these years and Paul Robinson saw it as the first period in the "modernization of sex."[14] Because there is no way of knowing whether this dramatic shift in attitudes affected the respondents, caution needs to be exercised about drawing conclusions from their answers.

A great deal of nineteenth-century prudery originated in the identification of women with virtue and of virtue with sexual purity. In a society that considered its women guardians of social morality, few things were more important than preserving their innocence. Therefore, in respectable circles, sex, childbirth, and the body were forbidden topics of conversation. When Emma Willard opened her female seminary in Troy, New York, in 1821, she shocked her contemporaries by including physiology in the curriculum. To maintain decorum, she pasted heavy paper over the illustrations of the human body.[15] Harriot Hunt thought that in "the important periods from thirteen to fifteen" girls should not go to school but "should stay at home, guided, guarded, [and] counselled by a mother. . . ."[16] In the sphere of dress, Victorian clothing effectively concealed the lower half of the female body. It was, indeed, considered the grossest impropriety to mention in mixed company that women had legs. Victorians even excluded females from their age-old role as midwives on the ground that witnessing childbirth would endanger their modesty and character. In 1818 a Boston physician wrote:

> It is obvious that we cannot instruct women as we do men in the science of medicine; we cannot carry them into the

> dissecting room and the hospital. . . . I venture to say, that a female could scarce pass through the course of education, requisite to prepare her as she ought to be prepared, for the practice of midwifery, without destroying those moral qualities of character, which are essential to the office.[17]

This protective concern inevitably extended to books; Shakespeare, for example, was considered much too lewd for women to read in unexpurgated editions.[18] Fanny Kemble, an English actress who married a Georgian plantation owner, thought that in some ways American society was even more restrictive than English. When she traveled from Philadelphia to Georgia, she noted in her diary, "the separation of men and women so rigidly observed by all traveling Americans took place . . . a most peculiar and amusing custom."[19] Frances Trollope commented on the social segregation of the two sexes.[20] In the same period, Tocqueville noted the extraordinary constraints placed on American wives, although he also observed that before marriage American girls were much freer than their peers in France.[21]

To the historian the nineteenth-century view of woman poses a perplexing interpretative problem, because it stands in direct opposition to traditional Western stereotypes. In a society marked by a self-conscious and aggressive Christianity, ministers and other arbiters of opinion discarded the image of woman as Eve, the source of individual and social evil, and replaced it with woman as the guardian of civilization. In *The Victorian Frame of Mind*, Walter Houghton attributed this transformation to romanticism and the need "to counteract the debasing influence on religion as well as morals of a masculine life preoccupied with worldly goods and worldly ambitions."[22] The latter observation begs the question, which is precisely *why* society turned to women, hitherto conceived as Eve, as a remedy for its moral problems. The reference to romanticism is not much more helpful because of the complexity of the movement described by this label. Many of the central impulses conventionally described as romantic undermine instead of encourage the ethos of domesticity. The insistence on the unity of flesh and spirit, the glorification of the physical and the emotional, the acceptance of all human drives as good, and the rejection of fixed social rules all emphasize the physical side of human nature, masculine and feminine, and legitimize sexuality without any reference to marriage.

The real source of the Victorian image of women was a secularized version of Puritan doctrines about love and marriage, which became influential among the middle classes in the eighteenth century and gradually transformed their attitudes toward females. Contrary to their reputation, the Puritans did not ignore the sexual impulse or underestimate the importance of physical relations in marriage. They accepted the sexual instinct as part of human nature and maintained that God meant it to be satisfied in matrimony. Women and men who did not marry would be tempted to sin. Therefore, unlike traditional Catholics, the Puritans condemned celibacy, couples who agreed to abstain from sexual relations after marriage, and wives or husbands who unilaterally left their mates' beds.[23]

Because they understood the importance of sexual compatibility in a successful marriage, the Puritans recognized that matrimony should be based on love and mutual attraction. Although they were too conservative to draw the logical conclusion, that young adults should be free to choose their own mates, they were uncomfortable with the traditional insistence on the unilateral right of parents to choose their offsprings' spouses. Puritan preachers constantly exhorted parents not to force their young into hateful matches and recommended long courtships to ensure that no natural repugnance existed between the couple. Love itself, they believed, followed marriage. Puritan ministers never confronted the problem of what to do if parents completely ignored their children's wishes or conceded the right of disobedience in extreme cases. In practice, however, Puritan influence usually resulted in giving children a veto over their parents' choices, if not the right to select their own mates actively. During the seventeenth century, this ill-defined, tenuous compromise spread beyond Puritan circles in both England and the colonies.[24] Although the young felt a strong obligation to obey their parents, letters, diaries, autobiographies, and biographies of the period all show that sons and daughters exercised their veto when they felt it necessary. Dorothy Osborne and William Temple, today probably the best-known English lovers of the period, both rejected repugnant matches but, at the same time, would not marry without their fathers' consent. Dorothy's letters reveal the deep conflict she felt about falling in love and committing herself to William in the face of both their families' opposition.[25] John Hutchinson was more fortunate. When he fell in love with Lucy Apsley, his father, an "honorably indulgent" parent, broke an advantageous match he had already arranged to suit his son.[26]

The Puritans worried about establishing marriage on the strongest possible foundation because they valued matrimony as the highest form of Christian life. The family that it created was the smallest unit in the godly commonwealth. Domestic prayer, family bible reading, and moral discipline in the home were all necessary to sanctify God's elect. So strong was the prejudice against single men in New England that towns often compelled bachelors to live with married men and their families.

Because of the importance they attached to matrimony, the puritans showed little tolerance for premarital or extramarital sexual relations. They regarded uncontrolled sexuality as a threat to the family and to the proper ordering of human affection, which should always give priority to love for God and obedience to his commands. Their views on confining sex to marriage were not new, but they were probably more rigorous in enforcing them than most other groups.[27] In seventeenth-century New England, the penalty for adultery was death, although the law was rarely enforced. Morgan attributes this leniency to the prevalence of offences of this type.[28]

Despite its powerful influence in early Stuart England, Puritanism never succeeded in imposing its standards on the entire community. Particularly in court and aristocratic circles, an easy tolerance of the double standard and sexual wrongdoing prevailed. Indeed, the moral split between Puritans and the court helped to undermine support for the monarchy in the crucial decades before the outbreak of revolution.[29]

The political defeat of Puritanism in the midseventeenth century led to a widespread reaction against the serious moralism that characterized the saints' approach to life. Their view of marriage as a romantic institution and insistence on sexual fidelity exerted less influence after the Restoration than before, again particularly among the aristocratic and upper classes. Charles II's promiscuous habits, the atmosphere of his court, and the importance of the "London Season" all contributed to the libertine tone of Restoration Society.

The character of aristocratic marriage in this period reinforced the trend away from Puritan moral standards. In this class matrimony functioned primarily as a social and economic liason between two families. Little concession was made to the Puritan view of marriage as a personal relationship that should be based on love. In his study of the English nobility from 1558 to 1641, Lawrence Stone maintained that Puritan attitudes toward marriage began to influence the peerage during the early seventeenth century and suggested that this influence grew stronger after the period he studied.[30] However, H. J. Habbakuk's work pointed convincingly in exactly the opposite direction.

Habbakuk maintained that after the Restoration the landed classes had to adjust to a society in which standards of expenditure were set by those whose wealth came from other sources than land, and in which taxation fell heavily on landowners. The landed classes responded by subordinating individual members of their families to the needs of their estates, exploiting the legal devices of entail and strict settlement to do so. They treated matrimony almost exclusively as a means of gaining and preserving landed wealth.[31] Historically arranged marriages and the double standard go together, since men will not agree to such matches unless they are free to pursue their sexual and romantic interests outside wedlock.[32] The late seventeenth and early eighteenth centuries were no exception to this pattern. The Puritan insistence on marital fidelity grew weaker as the trend toward arranged economic marriages grew stronger. George Saville, Marquis of Halifax, expressed the feelings of his age and class when he defended the double standard.

> Our sex seemeth to play the tyrant in distinguishing partially for ourselves, by making that in the utmost degree criminal in the woman which in a man passeth under a much gentler censure. The root and the excuse of this injustice is the preservation of families from any mixture which may bring a blemish to them . . . remember that next to the danger of committing the fault yourself the greatest is that of seeing it in your husband.[33]

Keith Thomas attributed the double standard not to the practical considerations discussed above, but "to the desire of men for absolute property in women, a desire which cannot be satisfied if the man has reason to believe that the woman has once been possessed by another man."[34] Although he noted the particular strength of this attitude among the upper classes, he did not explain *why* the prevalence of the double standard varied from one class to another.[35] He suggested, but did not develop, the idea, that it was connected to the system of arranged marriages among the landed classes, which encouraged the belief that women's chastity belonged to their fathers and husbands and was not their own to dispose of.[36] In my view this is the correct explanation. Through their doweries and inheritances, upper-class females conveyed property from their fathers to their husbands. Men therefore rightly associated their wives and daughters with wealth and counted them as economic assets. In such circumstances they easily acquired the habit of considering women—and their chastity— among their possessions. They were no more willing to share or give up control of this property than of any other.

The decline of Puritanism in the late seventeenth century was much more pronounced among the upper classes than among the middling ranks of society. Puritanism, known after the Restoration as nonconformity or dissent, survived among these groups. They retained the belief that matrimony should be based on love and that sex should be confined to marriage. They also preserved the Puritan ideal of husbands and wives as partners or helpmates, an ideal that often corresponded to economic reality, since many wives in this class worked alongside their husbands in their businesses and shops. Members of the middle classes regarded sexual passion as the major threat to their marital ideal and expressed negative attitudes toward it. They particularly associated destructive lust with upper-class men, who felt no compunction about preying on the wives and daughters of their social inferiors. The operation of the double standard ensured that males were the most obvious sexual offenders and that females frequently appeared to be the helpless victims of male passion. More and more, lust was associated with men, a complete inversion of traditional Western stereotypes.

By the eighteenth century, the idea had already appeared that marriage was a form of social discipline for unregenerate men, while women were more or less exempt from sexual feeling. Females elevated men morally in return for the economic security they gained through matrimony. In this period the respectable bourgeoisie considered it shocking for a woman to marry beneath her station because it showed she had surrendered to sexual passion, something considered quite "unnatural."[37] Dr. Johnson's widowed friend, Mrs. Thrale, appalled her admirers when she admitted to choosing her second husband, an Italian musician, for love.

The transition from this group of ideas to the female who stood at the center of the cult of domesticity was not difficult. All that was needed was to heighten and poeticize the belief in feminine asexuality and the woman's mission to elevate the more passionate male. The evangelical revival accomplished this in the late eighteenth century and early decades of the nineteenth. It also spread the cult of sexual purity and induced at least a portion of the upper class to accept codes of behavior that originated in the bourgeoisie.

The triumph of this middle-class ethos occurred in the decades that saw the triumph of the Industrial Revolution in England and the rise of the bourgeoisie to unprecedented economic and political power. The exclusion of middle-class women from the new industrial sector of the economy encouraged contemporaries to extend the contrast between masculine and feminine nature to sins flowing from materialism, greed, and competition. Males were conceived to be aggressive, selfish, tough, and lusty; females were passive, altruistic, weak, and sexless. Since the very survival of individual and social virtue depended on women, their natural purity had to be protected in the safe environment of the home. Thus, in the late eighteenth and early nineteenth centuries, economic and ideological movements converged to produce the image of females central to the cult of true womanhood.

In the colonies, Protestantism, often in its Puritan form, shaped basic attitudes toward marriage and sexual morality, but heterogeneous social and cultural conditions created regional variations within the common pattern. New England explicitly incorporated Puritan values and ideals, while the absence of a court or aristocracy prevented the emergence of an alternative code of behavior. In the South, attitudes toward marriage as an ideal state were very much like Puritan attitudes, but behavior often approximated the aristocratic model much more closely.[38] According to Spruill, economic considerations dominated the arranging of marriage and society readily tolerated male infidelity.[39] The sexual exploitation of female slaves by white men coexisted with an extravagant emphasis on white women's chastity. This pattern certainly encouraged both sexes to regard men as lustier than women and women as guardians of virtue. Since England supplied eighteenth-century Americans with most of their reading material, English novels, conduct books, and marriage manuals strongly influenced the colonists' views on marriage, women, and sex. Spruill's survey demonstrated that this literature exposed Southern colonists to both the secularized Puritan attitudes, which increasingly influenced the English middle classes, and the aristocratic values espoused by Halifax.[40]

Acceptance of the idea that women were more virtuous and less passionate than men became general in the first decades of the nineteenth century in connection with the Second Great Awakening and what Barbara Welter calls the "feminization of religion."[41] As men were swept up in the restless search westward for land, the early stages of industrialization, and the tumultuous politics of the Jacksonian era, they increasingly left the churches and care of their souls to women. It was a natural division of social function, given the increasing exclusion of middle-class women from the economy, their lack of political rights, and the existence of the belief that females were the purer sex. The association of women, religion, and the church reinforced the idea that they were ethically superior to men and the guardians of community morality. Ministers, who depended more and more on female congregations, united with them in the struggle against male sin. Since moral righteousness meant sexual purity, the women's new religious functions strengthened the belief that they were less tempted by strong instinctual drives.

The most important function of the morally superior nineteenth-century woman was bearing and raising children. In the Victorian period motherhood came to have the emotional and semisacred connotations that tempt one to write it with a capital "M." The mother's task was to care for her children physically, preserve their moral innocence, protect them from evil influences, and inspire them to pursue the highest spiritual values. If woman failed in this duty, she jeopardized the whole progress of civilization, an awesome responsibility indeed. The literature of female moral reformers reflected these beliefs about motherhood and called on mothers to destroy male sinfulness by indoctrinating their sons into a higher feminine morality.[42] This glorification of motherhood and exaggeration of its responsibilities was as new an element in Anglo-American culture as the opinion that females were particularly virtuous. Indeed, the two ideas evolved together and reinforced one another in eighteenth- and nineteenth-century thought.

The central thesis of Philippe Ariès' seminal work, *Centuries of Childhood,* is that new attitudes toward childhood and motherhood emerged in western Europe in the seventeenth and eighteenth centuries. In the early seventeenth century, child-rearing was not considered one of women's primary functions or surrounded with awesome moral responsibilities. Because relatively little prestige was attached to child-rearing, women who could afford them used wet nurses. In some cases, the infant was even sent to live with the nurse. Since using wet nurses made the woman much more available to her husband, upper-class men benefited

from, and probably advocated, these arrangements. Afflu-
ent women who nursed their children were considered ex-
amples of extraordinary maternal devotion.[43]

Whatever arrangements were made for the infant,
childhood ended much earlier than today. Youngsters entered the adult world long before puberty. Those destined
for a trade or craft were apprenticed anywhere between the
ages of 7 and 12 and were sent to live with their masters.
Parents in the lower classes placed their children in domestic service or some other menial job as soon as a position
could be found for them. In *The World We Have Lost,* Peter
Laslett observed that few children of the poor lived at
home.[44]

In England, even parents who could afford to keep
their children at home sent them to live with others. This
custom originated in the Middle Ages when placing a child
in the home of a patron of higher rank to be educated was
a way of climbing socially and providing for the child's
future. In the early Tudor period, an Italian visitor to England attributed the "putting out" of children to the "want
of affection" that he considered a national characteristic.[45]
The English themselves claimed that this practice ensured
that their children would be brought up better, since parents tended to be too indulgent with their own offspring.
Whatever the reason, the custom persisted among the upper classes in the Elizabethan and early Stuart periods. In
the 1570s, for example, Sir Robert Sidney wrote to his wife
Barbara about placing their two daughters:

> You know wel enough, whoe hath bin desirous to have them,
> and where they should bee as wel looked unto, as they can
> be in your own House, and more to their Good, and less to
> my charges. I meene for the Girls with my Lady of Hunting-
> don, and my Lady of Warwick, with whom also you told me
> you were willing to leave them. They are not so yong now,
> but that they may wel bee from their mother. Mary is almost
> ten, and Kate almost eight; and though I cannot find fault

hether unto, with their Bringing Up, yet I know every Day
more and more, it will bee fit for them to bee owt of their
Father's Hows. For heer they cannot learne, what they may
do in other Places; and yet, perhaps, take such Humors,
which, may be hurtful for them heerafter.[46]

The Puritans frequently "put out" their children, a custom
they carried with them to the colonies.[47] In the South,
planters frequently sent children in their teens abroad to be
educated, while the poor sent them to work or bound them
out at young ages.[48]

Even if children remained at home, their mothers
rarely had sole responsibility for them much beyond the
age of 7 years. They almost always lost control of boys at
this time. Male tutors took over among the rich, while
craftsmen, artisans, and peasants began to teach their sons
their skills. The upper classes often hired tutors and gover-
nesses for their daughters, too. In cases where girls were
not put out, mothers in all classes were responsible for
teaching them the domestic and managerial skills suited to
their station.[49] Whatever women's roles in child-rearing
after infancy, motherhood did not apparently carry much
importance with it. David Hunt has observed that in early
seventeenth-century France strong emotional ties between
mother and child were discouraged. Children belonged to
their fathers, who, in theory at least, made all the crucial
decisions about their education, career, and marriage.[50]
Levin Schüking maintains that in this period Puritan mothers performed few tasks in the family that their culture
considered important and that children showed little respect for them because they observed that they were less
well-educated than their mates and occupied a subordinate
place in the home.[51]

According to Ariès, attitudes toward children and
child-rearing practices began to change in the seventeenth
and eighteenth centuries. The innovators were influential
educators and churchmen who viewed childhood as a sepa-

rate stage of life in which the child should be segregated from the adult world and subjected to a special discipline. They advocated educational reforms based on these ideas and ultimately created the authoritarian boarding school of late seventeenth-century France. Ariès saw their efforts as part of the attempt of a small elite to impose order, hierarchy, and discipline on the turbulent world inherited from the Middle Ages. In every area institutional control over individual behavior increased. By the eighteenth century, the upper and middle classes had adopted the new view of childhood. They sent their children to the new boarding schools and attached a new importance to the role of the family in the child's moral training. Parents were particularly concerned to protect their children from sexual knowledge and experience, which they considered the major source of sin.

Puritans encouraged similar attitudes in English culture, since their view of the social order permitted neither the indifference to children nor their speedy absorbtion into the adult world that Ariès associated with the Middle Ages. One of the saints' major concerns was to impose discipline on human society. The family, the smallest unit in the commonwealth, played a key role in maintaining the social order established by God. Within its confines parents had to teach children the fundamentals of religion and to obey God's commandments. Above all, they had to prepare their children to receive divine grace should they be called.[52] In their view, breaking the child's will at an early age was necessary to achieve these goals.[53] Quakers in colonial America held very similar views.[54] The attitudes of both groups support Ariès' thesis that initially modern attitudes toward children involved greater repression of the young.

Child-rearing became an ever more important part of family life in the same centuries that the belief in female moral superiority was growing. The coincidence of these two strands of thought gave birth to the idea that mothers were particularly suited to assume the new ethical responsibilities vested in the home and family. This idea was a central element in the cult of domesticity and contributed to both its development and appeal.

To summarize, the cult of true womanhood was a compound of ideas—the restriction of the woman's proper sphere to the home, the moral superiority of females, and the idealization of her function as mother—which were relatively new elements in English and American culture. By the mid-nineteenth century, these conceptions prescribed the values and code of behavior that predominated among the middle classes and all those further down the social scale who aspired to respectability. The strength of this ideology derived from its apparent success in compensating women for the real loss in economic and political status and function that they suffered from 1800 to 1860. It made confinement to the home, which was deprived of many of its vital traditional functions, acceptable by assuring women that their presence as wives and mothers was necessary to preserve individual and social morality and save the nation from sin.

The influence of the cult of domesticity in mid-nineteenth-century America is not difficult for the historian to understand. What *is* difficult to understand is why the values it embodied defined American views of women well into the twentieth century. Despite enormous political, economic, social, and cultural change in the century after 1850, change that dramatically affected women, American ideas about females in the 1950s were remarkably similar to those of the Victorians. Betty Friedan's feminine mystique has a great deal in common with Barbara Welter's cult of true womanhood. This extraordinary continuity is due to the impact of Darwinism, the behavior of the first generation of college-educated and professional women, the conservative ideology of the woman's movement, the spread of doctrines of sexual liberation, and the influence of Freudianism. In one way or another they all helped to perserve the values central to the cult of domesticity and set the stage for the role conflicts so characteristic of twentieth-century American women.

From the 1860s Darwinism powerfully reinforced the influence of the cult of domesticity by justifying it in biological terms that were accepted as scientific truth. In the late nineteenth century, science replaced religion as the ultimate arbiter of truth in almost every area of human thought. Consequently, the persistence of the cult of true womanhood was encouraged by the fact that most Americans believed it to be based on a scientific view of feminine nature. Darwinism did not alter prevalent views of women; it gave them a new, up-to-date sanction.

Darwin asserted that evolution resulted from the survival of the more fit members of a species. The process of natural selection, as he called it, depended on chance variations within a species, which gave certain individuals a competitive advantage over others. Differences between the sexes developed in the same way. Men had a higher metabolic rate than women, which generated more variations and more agressiveness among males than occurred among females. Since natural selection depended on choice among different characteristics, the greater variation among men meant that they evolved more successfully into stronger and more intelligent beings than women. The specific mechanism that favored the survival of superior males was sexual selection. The female passively selected her mate by choosing the handsomer or stronger male. Over generations this produced offspring who possessed the advantageous characteristics of the successful suitors.

Motherhood increased women's disadvantages because it made them dependent on men. This dependence removed them to a certain extent from the progressive process of natural selection by linking their survival to the success or failure of their mates instead of to their own qualities in comparison with other women.

Since all sex-linked characteristics passed to the child from the parent of the same sex, boys inherited from their fathers the physical and mental advantages that resulted from the males' higher metabolic rate and greater contact with natural selection, while the girls of each generation started out further and further behind. According to Darwin, each parent transmitted non sex-linked traits to children of both sexes. However, all characteristics acquired after puberty were sex-linked and could be passed only to offspring of the same sex. Males inherited all sex-linked characteristics from their fathers, females from their mothers.

Women had less developed brains for the same reasons that they were less fit in all areas. A hierarchy of mental functions moved, in descending order, from reason to imagination to imitation to intuition to instinct. The more highly evolved male mind performed more efficiently at the higher range of this scale, the simpler female at the lower. The discovery by anthropologists that women's brains were smaller and less convoluted than men's seemed to confirm Darwin's theories.[55]

For 60 years or more after the publication of *The Origin of Species* in 1859, social scientists concerned with differences between the sexes thought almost exclusively in Darwinian terms. Many of them went even further than Darwin had in explaining human potential and behavior patterns by reference to instincts produced by evolution and independent of the social environment. One of the principal works on the subject, *The Evolution of Sex* by Patrick Geddes and J. Arthur Thomson, eliminated all social influences from its analysis of sex differences.

Despite the ascendancy of the cult of domesticity and Darwinism, the decades from 1860 to 1920 saw the entrance of women into institutions of higher education in large numbers and into the professions in tiny ones. By 1920, 47.3% of the total college enrollment was female, and women earned 33⅓% of the graduate degrees.[56] Patricia Graham attributed the revolution in female education to ideological pressure from the feminist movement, centered in the East, and the dire financial need of colleges and universities, which faced declining enrollments because of the Civil War, economic depression, and dissatisfaction with the college curriculum.[57] Much smaller numbers of females entered the professions in the same period. By 1920, 7.9% of the college professors, 3% of the lawyers, a small fraction of the doctors, and a handful of ministers were women.[58] The pressures against female professionals were much stronger than those against higher education for women. Because of the strength of the cult of domesticity, now reinforced by "science," choosing a career usually meant foregoing marriage and confronting family and social disapproval. Dorothy Mendenhall reported, for example, that after she entered Johns Hopkins Medical School, one of her aunts would not receive her socially and another referred vaguely to her "being south for the winter."[59] When M. Carey Thomas went to Leipzig to study for her Ph.D., her mother's friends considered it such a disgrace that they never mentioned her name again.[60] In the face of such disapproval, and the exaltation of the domestic role, most women inevitably preferred matrimony and maternity to a career. Furthermore, men did not welcome women into professions that they monopolized, and discriminated actively against them. Although individual females successfully surmounted these barriers, the problem was not solved as long as masculine self-interest and prejudice survived. The imposition of a quota on female entrance into medical schools for the first time in 1925, almost three-quarters of a century after the first women graduated, is a good example of the persistence of efforts to exclude them from the professions.

Although the females who went to college or entered the professions in this period were strong-willed noncon-formists, they tended to accept many of the assumptions of the cult of domesticity, particularly the incompatibility of the wife-mother role and a career. They did not attack this element of the cult of true womanhood frontally, but made choices within the parameters it defined. This can be seen in the marriage patterns of the first two generations of these women. Although 90 to 96% of the female popula-tion in the United States in the nineteenth century married, only 50 to 75% of the college-educated women did so. Fifty percent of the female doctors and 75% of the women who earned Ph.D.s between 1877 and 1924 remained single.[61] Females who were willing to become social pariahs in order to pursue the careers of their choice had internalized enough of the cult of true womanhood so that they ac-cepted the necessity of choosing between domestic and professional roles. Elizabeth Blackwell said explicitly that she decided to become a doctor to put a "strong barrier" between her and matrimony.[62] Both Angelina Grimké and Antoinette Brown Blackwell disappeared from the ranks of feminist leaders after their marriages, although in both cases their husbands were in favor of women's rights and careers. Alice Freeman Palmer resigned as President of Wellesley College when she married George Hubert Palmer, a philosophy professor at Harvard, in 1887. Pro-priety and ideology demanded that wives remain at home and, in many cases, domestic chores and childbearing drained them of energy that they might have devoted to intellectual activities or a career.

Furthermore, in the ultimate sense, Victorian culture made marriage unattractive at the same time that it exalted domesticity. Females raised to view sex as bestial often recoiled from matrimony if presented with an alternative pattern of life. Educated women, who could support them-selves, were obviously in the best position to exercise the

choice to remain single and avoid sexual intercourse altogether. As William O'Neill aptly queries, "Why beings as
pure as themselves should be subjected to the lusts of
men?"[63] Indeed, the whole contrast between male and
female nature and emphasis on female superiority created
a strong sense of solidarity among nineteenth-century
women. Many of them felt they had more in common with
each other than they ever could have with a man. Even
nonsexual contacts with males were bound to be degrad-
ing. The proliferation of women's clubs and reform groups
after 1870 drew on these feelings of sisterhood.[64] The
small group of females who attended women's colleges
lived for 3 or 4 years in relatively isolated communities that
encouraged intense ties among the students. One of the
attractions of the Settlement House Movement at the end
of the nineteenth century was undoubtedly that it enabled
these women to remain single and to continue to live together in relatively self-contained environments.[65]

A number of factors thus worked together to account
for the comparatively low marital rates of college-educated
and professional women from 1860 to 1920: social disapproval that made them unattractive to potential mates;
their own internalization of the cult of domesticity; and
their rejection of marriage on the basis of values embodied
in the cult of true womanhood itself. Whatever the relative
weight of these factors in the total picture, the important
point is that these women did not effectively attack the
current assumptions about the incompatibility of careers
and the wife-mother role. In this area, at least, they were
rather conservative pioneers. Their failure to raise the issue
contributed to the survival of the values embodied in the
cult of domesticity, while their marriage patterns meant
that later generations of American women, who turned to
them for inspiration, found a model of the single career
woman and virtually no guidance in how to combine the
professional and domestic roles.

The conservatism of the first generations of educated and professional women matched the conservatism of the woman's movement from 1870 to 1920. The founders of the American feminist movement, who adopted the Seneca Falls Resolutions of 1848, defined the woman's problem in the broadest possible sense. They believed that to achieve equality reforms were necessary in every area of life. As early as 1853, Elizabeth Cady Stanton remarked, "I do not know whether the world is quite willing or ready to discuss the question of marriage. . . . I feel, as never before, that this whole question of woman's rights turns on the pivot of the marriage relation, and, mark my word, sooner or later it will be the topic of discussion." Seven years later she reiterated, "How this marriage question grows on me. It lies at the foundation of all progress."[66] She saw that the real cause of inequality between the sexes was rooted in ideas about female nature and a multitude of social and economic institutions and relationships that assumed and depended on the subordination of women. Therefore, drawing on the egalitarian philosophy of the enlightenment, she launched a sweeping attack on the cult of domesticity and all its assumptions. For her, deprivation of the vote was not the core of the problem.

Unfortunately, the feminist movement lost this broad perspective in the last quarter of the nineteenth century. It focused increasingly on the issue of the vote and paid less and less attention to economic opportunity or issues related to the domestic sphere. From a tactical point of view, this was good strategy, since a wide spectrum of women agreed on the vote. It could be advocated without challenging pervasive assumptions about woman's nature and separate male and female spheres. In this period suffragists argued for the vote on the ground that women were different from and even superior to men, instead of on the ground that the two sexes were fundamentally the same. Females should have the vote so they could contribute their

special capacities, talents, and point of view to society.[67]
Stanton's egalitarian ideology was thus discarded for arguments based on the Victorian notion that women were biologically and tempermentally different from men. Even
Ellen Dubois, who emphasized the radicalism of the woman's suffrage movement, observed that "the doctrine of
separate sexual spheres was supreme in the nineteenth century and even suffragists were unable to challenge certain
basic aspects of it. Most notably, they accepted the particular suitability of women to domestic activities and therefore
their special responsibility for the private sphere. . . ."[68]
The character of the women's rights movement as it
evolved meant that in the period of its greatest influence,
feminists fought almost exclusively for the vote and
avoided attacking the fundamental assumptions of the cult
of domesticity. Therefore, despite the passage of the nineteenth amendment in 1920, Victorian views of women survived.

The "sexual revolution" of the early twentieth century
and the triumph of ideas preaching female sexual liberation
had less influence on the ideological status quo than might
be expected. Propagandists for sexual freedom encouraged
females to accept the idea of a unique feminine character
that suited them for special—and surprisingly traditional—
functions. This group included Havelock Ellis, Edward
Carpenter, and Ellen Key. Ellis was a British physician who
believed in feminine distinctiveness and superiority. In his
best-selling treatise, *Man and Women,* he described females
within the parameters of Darwinist theory. He believed, for
example, that due to their physiological constitutions,
women were both less variable and more emotional than
men. He especially stressed the importance of the men-
strual cycle. It influenced feminine strength, intelligence,
and dexterity so that women's abilities fluctuated with their
monthly cycle. Menstruation particularly affected their
powers of self-control. In Ellis' view, this monthly cycle

raised questions about the fitness of females for business positions.

As a Darwinist, Ellis integrated both men and women into the animal kingdom. In this context, he asserted that women were as sexually passionate as men. He even argued that some of their ostensible intellectual inferiority was due to the extraordinary inhibitions resulting from the sexual repression on which society insisted. Despite comparable levels of passion, male and female sexuality were, according to Ellis, very different in character. Sexual differences extended to every aspect of behavior. Therefore, although he called for an unprecedented liberation of female sexuality, Ellis emphasized the differences between males and females and analyzed women in terms of their biological character.[69]

Ellen Key, an outspoken advocate of free sexual expression for women, thought they should concentrate on love and motherhood, the two spheres most suited to their nature. According to Key, a mature female was completely devoted to maternity. On these grounds, she opposed the suffrage movement, the campaign for legal equality, and the feminist insistence on women's right to work.[70] Her contemporary, Margaret Sanger, also urged females to seek power in their own spheres and concentrate on the distinctive "feminine element." One of the reasons she advocated contraception was that it would liberate female sexuality.[71] The net effect was to recognize female sexuality (admittedly an important gain) while leaving intact the dichotomy between the female-private and male-public spheres.

The reception and dissemination of Freudian psychoanalytic theory between 1920 and 1950 completed the process that preserved nineteenth-century views of women in terms that made them acceptable in the twentieth century. Freud and his followers prescribed traditional roles for women and defended customary attitudes toward them in up-to-date, scientific terminology.[72] To Freud the first crucial experience in the formation of the female personality was penis envy, an emotion little girls felt as soon as they noticed that little boys had something that they lacked. Girls wanted a penis because it was superior for masturbation, although Freud did not make clear how they knew this. Because of their deficiency, girls had contempt for their own bodies and an inferiority complex. Out of anger at their mothers, whom they blamed for their lack, they turned to their fathers in the hope that they would supply them with the missing organ and entered what Freud called the oedipal stage. When daughters realized their fathers could not fulfill this wish, they developed a substitute desire to bear the father's babies. In psychoanalytic terms, the baby was a substitute for the penis. In adulthood, normal women transferred this desire from their fathers to another man. It was natural for females to desire maternity; if they did not, it was because they were suffering from unresolved penis envy and a masculinity complex. Intellectual and professional ambitions in women stemmed from penis envy.

Freud also traced tempermental differences between men and women to biology. Femininity was essentially passive, masochistic, and narcissistic. Divergence from this norm, a restatement of Victorian prescription in scientific terminology, was unhealthy. Modesty and jealousy, both peculiarly feminine traits, originated in penis envy.

The difference between the childhood Oedipus complex in boys and girls, again rooted in biology, accounted for the differing development of the male and female superego or conscience. The boy, who had a penis, feared castration and developed a superego to conceal and transcend his anxiety. Since the girl lacked a penis to begin with, she had no stimulus for developing a superego, which explained her lack of moral sense and idea of justice, as well as her subjection to emotional bias instead of judgment.

The female's weak superego[73] and an inferior capacity for sublimating her libido (i.e., sex drive) explained why women have contributed little to civilization and culture in the past and have little hope of doing so in the future. The female was less able to sublimate than the male because she possessed a weaker libido to start with.[74] Her involvement in pregnancy and childbirth also undermined her capacity for sublimation.[75] In *Civilization and Its Discontents*, Freud postulated an inherent opposition between women and culture.[76] Finally, he maintained that repressive sexual patterns carried over into every area of the woman's life and explained her unquestionable intellectual inferiority. These repressive patterns began in childhood, when the girl gave up masturbation in the period of penis envy, and were reinforced by the whole character of her upbringing.[77]

Because of the female's weak libido, men had to take the initiative in sexual relations to insure continuation of the race, although this was hardly consistent with Freud's conviction that normal women desired maternity. Sexual aggressiveness was natural and appropriate to men, sexual passivity to women. Freud also maintained that intercourse was painful to women and any sexual pleasure they felt was masochistic.[78] Although his language was different, there was really little distinction between Freud's woman and the Victorian stereotype.

Freudianism and modern views of female sexuality combined with assumptions about the women's sphere inherited from the nineteenth century to form what Andrew Sinclair called the "New Victorianism" and Betty Friedan the "feminine mystique."[79] The continuity between nineteenth- and twentieth-century views of women has added enormously to their social and cultural impact in the period since World War II. This continuity has created the illusion that American females have always performed the functions and filled the roles that the feminine mystique assigned them. Until the rebirth of feminism in the 1960s shattered public consensus on the subject, women who tried to combine careers with their roles as wives and mothers did so in the face of assertions that they were disregarding their historic functions and imperiling civilization.[80] Many of them had internalized prevailing doctrines about their sex and consequently carried an enormous psychic and emotional burden as they tried to manage their domestic and professional lives.

This chapter has shown that women have not been full-time mothers throughout history and that the home was not considered the peculiarly feminine sphere until the economy moved out of it. Both the cult of domesticity and the view of female nature on which it rested developed relatively recently in Anglo-American culture. History teaches neither that females have always been full-time mothers nor that they have always been separated from the productive economy. It teaches, instead, that these patterns evolved as an adjustment to modern, industrial society. It also opens the liberating prospect that just as ideas about women changed to suit the early industrial world, they can do so now in response to the needs and conditions of postindustrial society. The effort of contemporary feminists to break the connection between women, the home, and child-rearing can succeed, and professional women in late twentieth-century America can at long last be freed from their burden of guilt and anxiety.

Chapter 4

SOME INNER CONFLICTS OF WOMEN IN A CHANGING SOCIETY

Esther Menaker, Ph.D.

It is a truism that what we become psychologically—how we think of ourselves, how we function with others, how fulfilled or frustrated we are—depends to some extent on the social, economic, and historical circumstances in which we find ourselves and to some extent on what we, as unique individuals, bring to the situation. Yet this acknowledgment that both nature and nurture influence our lives, upon closer examination, reveals to us an intricately woven fabric of interacting psychological processes. Because we are children of the past, striving in the present either to detach ourselves from it or to integrate it with our ideals for the future, we are to some extent in constant psychological movement and therefore inevitably, to some degree, in conflict. This is especially true at a time of social change when new opportunities and responsibilities, new expectations and pressures give rise to the need for new adaptations—adaptations not only in the overt sense of daily functioning, but inner adaptations of a psychological nature. It is to these inner processes in relation to women that I address myself.

The social changes that have affected women and that, in fact, women have to a large extent helped to create, are part of a worldwide movement for liberation by peoples who have been historically discriminated against either because of race, color, sex, religion, or economic position. One meaning of liberation is obvious; it is liberation from economic and social disadvantage, from squalor, poverty, degradation, and despair. But there is an additional, psychological meaning of the term liberation; it is freedom from a socially assigned role that had inhibited the optimum fulfillment of the individual's capabilities. It is in this latter sense that social change is of special importance to women. The traditionally assigned role of wife and mother that had previously been limited to the domestic functions associated with these roles has given way to a broader conception of woman as person. As a "person," woman might fulfill herself in many ways; these might include being wife and mother, but would encompass participation in the work world outside the home. Sometimes work means a serious commitment to a career; sometimes it means either economic independence or the ability to contribute to the economic well-being of a family; sometimes it means gratification in the actual function of the work as well as the social satisfaction that contact with others can bring. Whatever its meaning, the opportunities that have been created for women through social change for work and participation in the life of the community have changed not only her actual functioning, but her image of herself. And it is the changed self-conception, the new hopes and expectations of life, that come into conflict with that part of the self-image that derives from an identification with the mother, who generally stands for the traditional role of woman.

We are all tied to the past, to tradition, through an identification with parents. Every small child begins to be a person in his or her own right first, by imitating the behavior, attitudes, feelings, and thoughts of those closest to him or her—usually his or her parents. Gradually these imitations become internalized, and the child *is* to some extent like the parents or, as is sometimes the case, just the opposite of a particular parent. This tendency to counteridentification, to a sometimes almost conscious decision not to repeat the life-style or personality of a parent, is particularly common among little girls who have repudiated the traditional feminine role as their mothers have lived it. Clinical experience with young women in recent years has made it clear that a major factor in this repudiation is the little girl's experience of her mother's unhappiness, her lack of fulfillment, her bitter feeling that life has cheated her and, above all, her low opinion of herself. In this depreciated self-image, the mother has accepted the male-oriented social attitude toward woman as an inferior, as a second-class citizen. Thus she not only thinks poorly of herself, but looks on her daughter with a mixture of pity and condescension, of disappointment and yet hope that her daughter's lot may be better than her own. And should it indeed prove to be better, the mother's feelings are inevitably tinged with envy. This mixture of conflicting feelings on the mother's part, and the daughter's need to detach herself from the mother, generally result in strife between mother and daughter in the actuality of their daily lives and in confusion, tension, and burdensome guilt in the inner psychological life of the daughter.

If, on the other hand, the mother's attitude toward her daughter's aspirations is predominantly positive and affirmative, she inspires much less of the rebellious, counteridentificatory response; the daughter therefore can much more contentedly identify with the feminine role of woman and mother as represented by the personality of her mother, and can pursue her vocational or career interests at the same time.

For many women, fulfillment of self involves satisfaction on two fronts: the biologically creative front that seeks gratification in a sexual relationship and its ultimate outcome in motherhood, and the ego-creative front in which the individual's unique personality is expressed in work efforts of some sort. The second need is in no way a repudiation of femininity nor an expression of masculine wishes as Freudian theory would have us believe. It is a natural manifestation of individuation that until recently has had little chance for expression because woman was subjected by society to an assigned role. In an article that is now timely, but was written many years ago, Otto Rank understood the basic wish of all human beings to be that which they are. He, therefore, disagreed with Freud's theory regarding woman's "masculinity complex" and wrote of woman that she "has always wanted and still wants first and foremost to be a woman, because this and this alone is her fundamental self and expresses her personality, *no matter what else she may do or achieve.*"[1] The last part of this sentence is of extreme importance, because it emphasizes the fact that it is not the nature of the activity that defines an individual in terms of his or her psychobiological role. Our conception of what is feminine or masculine is socially conditioned, but does not reflect the inner feeling of an individual about himself or herself except as he or she is conditioned by social stereotypes. For example, because of custom and tradition, we have thought of engineering as a masculine occupation and therefore unfeminine, or of the artist as effeminate and therefore not masculine. These are social stereotypes that are passed down from parents to children and that influence an individual's self-conception to the extent that he or she is emotionally bound to parents or to the social community. But the more autonomous (or sometimes rebellious) an individual is, the less will the socially stereotypic role definition be reflected in his or her self-image.

Historically, a change in social values that generally means the loss of old values, whether it results from dislocation of populations, change in political or economic structure, or the opening up of new opportunities for social and economic improvement or for greater self-expression, inevitably results in conflict for the individual. The individual is caught in the paradox of the discrepancy between the desired liberation and advancement and the resultant loss of security. This is not to say that we should eschew social progress or the opening up of new opportunities for individuals; we could not even if we would, because social processes are in constant movement and flux. But we must be clear that the benefits of positive social change bring with them certain psychological problems.

For woman the opening up of new opportunities for work away from home can represent, at one and the same time, the realization of a longed-for ego-ideal of liberation and fulfillment as well as a loss of continuity with the traditions of the past. But this loss is far from abstract, since the traditional ego-ideal is embodied in the mother and becomes, in the course of maturation, incorporated into the personality of the daughter. It is, therefore, a psychological reality, an actual part of the daughter, even though, in the name of new goals, it lies dormant and unexpressed in the daily life of the individual. The young woman, therefore, who has synthesized a new and independent ego-ideal out of the social influences that impinge on her, has separated from her mother as well as from a part of herself. In such separation there is always the implication of rejection, and for this rejection there is always guilt. This need not be an overriding guilt; unless it reaches neurotic proportions, it need not seriously inhibit a woman's functioning either in her work or emotional life. But it must be carried as a part of one's emotional baggage.[2]

The awareness of guilt feelings on the part of a woman who is committed to a career as well as to being a wife and mother often surfaces in relation to her children. She is oversensitive to echoes of the socially prescribed role of the traditional mother as they might be heard in some implications that she does not spend sufficient time with her children. She begins to measure her devotion in terms of time spent, losing the certainty of her emotional attachment to her children as it is experienced in spontaneous feeling. She is a ready victim of the latest psychological nostrums on child-rearing, often replacing common sense with the illusion that there is some perfect and correct way to raise children. If she could only follow the proper prescription, she would produce the perfectly happy and well-adjusted child—a tribute to her maternal devotion and an expiation of her guilt.

Let me not be misunderstood. The issue of guilt does not arise out of the dual role of woman—career and motherhood. The task of coordinating these two facets of life may indeed provide opportunity for attaching guilt to specific logistical problems in the working out of two roles; but guilt does not arise from the duality itself. It is an inner psychological phenomenon that takes place within a social context and is socially conditioned only to the extent that societal values correspond to internalized values that the individual has taken over from parents. Clearly, if the social attitude toward the dual role of woman is affirmative, her conflict will be lessened and her ability to act on her aspirations will be heightened. This is the positive outcome of the changes in the social and economic position of women that we are witnessing today.

However, the psychological source of feelings of guilt that so many women experience lies primarily in the relationship to the mother. A woman's resolve to be different from her mother, to choose a different life-style, to be both wife and mother and to have a career, and to challenge her mother's values, her social attitudes, even her child-rearing practices—these come in conflict with what she had "learned" from her mother and help to create feelings of uncertainty and guilt.

The psychological separation from the mother need not necessarily take place in the overt choice of a dual-role life-style; it may come about in a woman's determination to be a better wife and mother than she felt her own mother to be. This is especially the case when a woman's memory of her own childhood is one of emotional deprivation, or if she perceived the relationship between her parents to have been a stressful and unhappy one. When such conditions exist and the mother is rejected as a role model, there is hostility in the rejection above and beyond that which accompanies every separation. It is hostility for lack of love, for deprivation. Yet despite the fact that the young woman consciously feels justified in her anger toward her mother, she often experiences guilt—a guilt that arises from the fact that as a small, dependent child she incorporated her mother's values, her mother's ways, and her mother's rejection and condemnation of her. These feelings are now her own. Perhaps her mother was right; perhaps she is really the selfish, disobedient, inconsiderate, and incompetent individual at whom her mother had pointed a finger when she was a child. A repressed self-hatred unconsciously resides within her, and it emerges when she herself becomes a mother. She finds that she cannot easily, nor always, be the "corrected" mother that she so consciously determined to be. The stresses of the maternal experience, the frustrations and disappointments that are inevitable in all human relationships evoke the old, original identification with her mother. She finds herself critical of and impatient with her children, and she hates herself with the same vigor with which she hated her mother for her lack of love and attention and for her belittlement of herself and of her daughter.

This psychological pattern that I have just described is very common; it is practically an inevitable aspect of the struggle between generations. Except in the most rigidly structured and traditional societies, each new generation seeks to separate from its antecedents by placing the stamp of its own individual ethos on its behavior, its values, its commitment to social change, and its special view of progress. The opportunity to do just this is obviously greater in times of social change and in societies whose structure is open-ended. It follows, therefore, that today women who are able to take advantage of the opportunities for the fulfillment of new, self-chosen roles and individual ego-ideals, especially if they have chosen a dual role, may find the inner psychological conflict with the imprint left on them by their mothers especially poignant.

As an illustration of this point, the case of a young woman whom I treated some years ago comes to mind. I have spoken of her elsewhere[3] in a somewhat different but related connection. However, since that time, the unhappy crises that developed in her life bring into even more dramatic relief than before her struggle to separate psychologically from her mother and to consolidate a new identity. Her life, viewed now over a longer period during which she became a mother and experienced separation from her husband and the threat of serious illness, illustrates the "return of the repressed" as well, because the old identifications with her mother came to the surface at times of crisis and caused her great conflict, depression, and loss of self-esteem.

Jeanne, as I have called my patient, "grew up" in a tradition-bound home of immigrant parents in a community in which her family belonged to a minority group. Her parents had rigid ideas about the role of a young woman. She was expected to marry at an early age and raise a family. Higher education or a career of any kind for a young lady were frowned on. To Jeanne, however, the opportunities of the larger *milieu* beckoned. She had literary talent and was determined to make a career for herself as a writer. That she might have to repeat her mother's limited life terrified her. It was in some measure this anxiety that, added to the normal impulse toward fuller self-realization, was responsible for the great efforts that she made to get an education and training for her chosen field.

The social environment in which she grew up, as distinguished from the environment of her immediate family, offered Jeanne these opportunities. She broke out of the traditional, assigned role of her familial culture, acquired a good education, and ultimately found work in the field of journalism. There was a price to be paid, as there inevitably is, for this piece of psychosocial progress. Jeanne suffered from acute anxiety and a tendency toward depression. These were her reasons for seeking psychotherapeutic help. It is not surprising that the difficulty in synthesizing conflicting identifications within her ego structure—those stemming from her early relationship to her mother and those arising from the social *milieu* that offered her the opportunity to choose her own individual pathway—should have led to anxiety. The subjective feeling was always one of uncertainty. "Will I make it? Will I succeed?" thought Jeanne. It is such uncertainty that unavoidably accompanies social change. It is not that social change causes anxiety in a primary sense, but that when it supports the inner processes of separation and individuation, it augments the initial conflicts with parental figures.

Jeanne's therapy, by implicitly granting permission for a new definition of self and a new role as a woman, largely through the establishment of an identification with her therapist, enabled her to overcome much of her anxiety. She did succeed in her work, which offered her the chance for some creative expression, and she was no longer depressed. In addition, she overcame her sexual prudery (a heritage of her childhood upbringing), and at an appropriate age married a man for whom she felt genuine love and affection. Her family had scarcely outgrown the contractual conception of arranged marriages, so that Jeanne's choice of a mate in terms of individual expressiveness represented a great advance both in social and psychological terms over the expressive capacities of her parents.

For approximately 8 years her marriage was a good one. Then certain specific stresses impinged on inner, more unconscious emotions and aroused conflicts in herself and her husband that the marriage could not withstand. Her first child was a daughter, much loved by both parents and posing no threat to their relationship. However, a second pregnancy eventuated in a stillbirth and, for Jeanne, the ensuing unhappiness and depression that this loss precipitated caused a regression to early identifications with her mother. In her marriage she began to repeat her mother's pattern of interaction with her husband: carping, complaining, denigrating, belittling. A hostile dissatisfaction, an aggressive frustration, cast a pall over her marital relationship. She was conscious of the repetition of her mother's pattern of behavior and of her mother's angry feeling toward men, and she was filled with self-loathing for having regressed to an emotional position that she had struggled so hard to overcome.

It was in this atmosphere of marital tension, belittled self-image, and depression that she again became pregnant and, in due time, gave birth to a son. The birth of a boy, for reasons that are irrelevent to this discussion, threatened her husband's emotional security. He was unprepared to be father to a son, at least within the framework of a marriage that was souring under the impact of Jeanne's querulousness and ready hostility. Within less than a year after the boy's birth, he left the family.

It was the circumstance of her having been deserted that caused Jeanne to consult me again, and it was in this second installment of her treatment that the mechanism of regression to her earliest identifications became increasingly apparent. When the realization that her marriage was over was finally accepted, Jeanne began to go out with other men. In these relationships she showed a tendency to be childish and demanding, like her mother. With her children she became more irritable and impatient and experienced them as an interference with her social life. Here again was a repetition of her mother's attitude toward her own children, toward whom she was at once possessive yet disinterested. Needless to say, the pull back into her mother's ways filled Jeanne with self-hatred, criticality, and depression. Unfortunately, life dealt her still another blow in the form of a serious illness in the course of which the old patterns were still further reinforced.

It is not my present purpose to go into the details of Jeanne's various relationships or of her interaction with her children. Her awareness of the regression to an identification with her mother and her self-criticism of this regression kept her from becoming a duplicate of her mother. Economic necessity, to some extent, dictated her life-style. She was fortunate in finding a position in her own field of

writing that enabled her to continue work and motherhood, kept her in touch with the larger world outside her
home, and gave her satisfaction in the realization of her
independence and competence. She would not be caught
in a permanent regression to old identifications largely because she had tasted the satisfactions of a freely chosen
life-style. The superimposed new identifications, although
not completely or securely synthesized with other aspects
of her ego, nevertheless left enough of a mark to insure the
functioning of her personality in the name of different ego-
ideals and a different value system than that which had
dominated her mother's life and personality. It was social
change and the opportunity that it created for the adoption
of a new self-definition that provided the soil in which new
identifications could develop; it was psychotherapy that
gave form and substance to these identifications.

The significance of Jeanne's life story lies in the fact
that it points out the struggle to consolidate a new identity
in the face of the impact of two opposing tendencies: first,
the pull of early identifications with a mother who offered,
as a model, the traditional mother-wife role; and second,
the opportunity for a new role combining the satisfactions
of marriage and motherhood with those of career. In general, the intensity of this conflict for the individual young
woman depends on a number of things: the initial strength
of her own ego and the vitality of her will to be separate and
individuated and to resist unwelcome social pressures; her
relationship to her father and siblings; the availability of
persons in the environment who might offer ego-ideals to
be emulated that differ from those of her family; and perhaps above all the nature of her relationship to her mother.
If the mother affirms the dual-role aspirations of her
daughter either because she herself has lived her life in this
way or because she would have wished to have done so, the
conflict of identifications for the young woman is much
reduced. She is able to identify with her mother's positive

expectations, which are in harmony with her own wishes for self-realization, and therefore to avail herself freely of the opportunities for work, profession, or career that a changing society offers her.

I have emphasized the role of the mother in the formation of a young woman's identity mainly because identification with her is the child's earliest primary identification—one that grows out of the child's first relationship. For the daughter who must consolidate a sexual identity as a woman with one involving her social, intellectual, and professional functioning, this primary identification with her mother is crucial because she is of the same sex as her mother. However, the role of the father in the young girl's development should not be minimized. What he is as a person, what he represents as an ego-ideal, and how he relates to his daughter all have a great impact on the development of her personality. It is important for her sexual identity that her father love and admire her as a little girl with the potentiality for becoming an attractive woman; and for her ego development it is important that he affirm her goals and aspirations. Often these goals derive from the daughter's identification with her father's vocation, with his achievements, and with his code of behavior in relation to others. To the extent that the father encourages such identifications, especially if they are consistent with her striving for autonomous expressiveness and are realizable in action in the outside world, will the daughter's synthesis of a secure identity be made easier. Indeed, it is the affirming love of a father that makes possible for the daughter the choosing of a husband who will in his turn support the dual-role identity of his wife, should that be her aspiration.

In a period of social change in which the position and psychology of women is changing, the role of men must also change. What is noticeable today on the part of men of the current generation of marriageable age is paradoxically either a flight and withdrawal from any significant or permanent commitment to a relationship with a woman or, having entered marriage, an increased involvement and participation in the life of the family. It is this latter supportive attitude that obviously frees the woman to choose and achieve a dual-role identity with much less conflict. In this way man participates, not only in the liberation of woman, but in a progressive process of social change.

Although this chapter is specifically concerned with the kind of inner conflict in women that is sometimes augmented by a society in transition, I would not like to leave the theme of the relationship between social change and individual psychology without pointing out that what is herein described is a general phenomenon of which the psychology of woman is only one example. Whenever the traditional identifications representing the values, ego-ideals, or self-conceptions of individuals or groups are impinged on by differing values, a conflict arises between the impulse to adhere to the early identifications and the striving to absorb the new values, especially if these promise greater fulfillment in the realm of self-realization. This has been observed by anthropologists and sociologists when studying phenomena such as cross-cultural influences, the migrations of peoples, immigration to new countries, the loss of or change in religious belief, and changes in sexual mores or in moral values. The exposure to what is in essence a new environmental influence in the form of some sort of social change and the need to adapt to it is reflected in the inner psychological life of individuals as a conflict in the area of those identifications that regulate the values and self-conceptions that determine the nature of behavior. Sometimes the conflict is so profound and so unbalancing that it may result in a personality disturbance so extreme that it produces severe neurosis, psychosis, or even criminal behavior. Thus social change may too readily become social upheaval, and that which inaugurated the constructive development of greater freedom and self-expressiveness for individuals may herald a destructive imbalance in their psychic lives. We can only guard against this latter outcome through the awareness of the pressures of internalized conflict and the knowledge that these pressures can be eased by the establishment early in life of loving and flexible identifications that can withstand the onslaught of new ways and new values. In the development of woman, for whom the structuring of personality is particularly complex because of her dual role (her need to be true to her self as well as to her biological role), the quality of the early identifications with both parents is crucial. Therefore, not only for her own sake, but for the well-being of society, is it important that parents deviate from historical precedent and express a special love and affirmation of their daughters.

Chapter 5

FEMALE IDENTITY SYNTHESIS

Doris Bernstein, M.A.

We are confronting a cultural upheaval in which the familiar models of masculinity and femininity do not seem viable. In our era many social institutions are in flux; church, state, army, and schools are losing their powerful functions as advisors and protectors. Now traditional models of femininity and masculinity as aids and organizers of developing personalities are crumbling. Educational and career opportunities for women, smaller families, distant families, and divorces are all creating new realities and making new demands on men and women. Ready-made societal solutions to old conflicts are not available, and individuals must find new solutions.

In a sense, the newly emerging demands on the individual are unprecedented; we are asking that each individual find a way to encompass within his or her own ego boundaries and his or her own identity all instinctual derivatives so that each individual will be active, passive, assertive, receptive, and aggressive as the need arises. These changes are evident in clinical work as women are moving into new spheres of activity and are trying to integrate new aspirations with more traditional concepts of themselves as women.

In working with women, I have found them struggling in roles for which there are few precedents. The models of "femininity" that were presented to them during their childhood do not fit their current adult lives. Most women I have treated were expected to live lives much like those of their mothers (i.e., to be wives and mothers in turn). While many were well-educated, they were expected to make use of their education only until they married or in case of financial emergency. In order to meet the challenge of new demands it is necessary that women find a new identity synthesis.

I use the phrase "identity synthesis" instead of "identity" to convey the ongoing process of synthesizing identity components such as gender identity, ego, superego, ideals, and identifications; the concept encompasses a sense of self, a sense of continuity with one's past and an orientation toward the future.

Every culture provides identity models that are crystallized out of the total range of human feelings, wishes, needs, and aspirations. These models serve society adaptively by meeting cultural needs; they serve the child growing up in the culture as a guide and goal for developing an adaptive character.[1]

Developmental conflicts and early and often unconscious identifications and repressions can facilitate or inhibit later adaptive adult identity experiences. Psychoanalysis, through its study of the child and character formation, can contribute to the understanding of the vicissitudes of childhood out of which a sense of identity emerges.

Freud viewed the emergence of femininity and masculinity as outcomes of the interaction of manifestations of physiological bisexuality and varied identifications as consolidated at the time of the resolution of the oedipal period. Femininity was dependent on the repression of the "masculinity" in the girl's character and on appropriate identifications with her mother. The boy's masculinity required the reverse—repression of "femininity" and his identifications with the father. The male repressed his wish to be nurturing and some of his wishes to be nurtured and projected them onto his wife, whose role was to be dependent on him and, at the same time, care for many of his needs. The woman repressed her aggressive, assertive strivings and projected them onto her husband, who was required to be strong, to work, and to provide economically for her. Through these mechanisms of selective repression and mutual projection and the resulting unconscious gratification, masculinity and femininity are defined.

The roles thus defined could be relevant, adaptive, and even mutually gratifying in a culture that was stable and in a marriage that was stable, but they can no longer be adaptive, at least for women, in the changing world of today. The woman who has repressed her assertive, aggressive impulses and has developed her personality along this model often finds herself inadequately equipped to work, to be a divorcée or a widow, or to make her way in the world after child-rearing years (the empty nest syndrome). Confronted with new demands, it is necessary for her to attempt a major reorganization of herself and to create a new identity synthesis.

Autonomy, independence, and assertiveness, the qualities most valued in our society, are considered "unfeminine."[2] Women face a dilemma; in order to be feminine, they must relinquish the very character traits and repress the underlying instinctual drives that they later need to develop their own potential or even to survive. These traits are admirable in women only when they are exercised in the service of others' needs. In homemaking and child-rearing, these qualities are permissible and make the woman who exercises them a "good" woman in her own internal system and in the eyes of the outside world. When she ventures to use them in behalf of her own personal interests or pursuits, however, she loses esteem and "femininity." When a woman is called "independent," it is usually in a perjorative tone.

Women are often very anxious in situations that call for aggressive action because aggression is an impulse that has had to be repressed in the developing girl. As their lives are requiring them to behave more assertively, this childhood repression is maladaptive. Women's efforts to cope with this issue are clearly manifest in the assertiveness training groups that have become very popular on a national scale. Men, in response to the changes, are also confronted with considerable anxiety. As they are being asked to take over some of the nurturing toward themselves and their children, they, too, are confronted with a repressed forbidden aspect of themselves. If we consider the resistance by both men and women to the Women's Liberation Movement, it is apparent that anxiety or rage have been generated. The movement undermines the underlying personality structures of both men and women.

I am going to discuss three aspects of female development that I have found contribute to difficulties women are having in the face of the change in values and social patterns in our culture. I will discuss (1) problems in separation-individuation; (2) the nature and contents of the female superego; and (3) problems in forming identifications as they influence the adult identity synthesis.

1.   SOME ISSUES IN SEPARATION-INDIVIDUATION

The first aspect of female identity synthesis that I discuss is the separation-individuation process.[3] There can be no satisfactory individual identity experience if the child does not develop an awareness of itself as a being physically and emotionally separate from the mother. The establishment and maintenance of psychic individuation, together with core gender identity,[4] forms the basis of the identity experience.[5]

It is often said that women are lacking independence and autonomy, that they are dependent on others, and that they lack individuality and are "followers." Women tend to be defined and to define themselves in terms of their relationships to others. The female is always somebody's object; first she is Mommy's baby doll, then Daddy's darling, later someone's wife, and then someone's mother. This immediately brings into focus a core problem with women; they find it difficult to define themselves without these references.

Those who emphasize social factors will point to cultural pressures on women to remain dependent, even somewhat helpless and childlike, in order to be womanly.

Psychoanalysis has stressed the inner conflicts that interfere with individuation. However, I have found it is the
fitting or convergence of outer pressures with these inner
struggles that make the individuation process difficult for
girls.

I will discuss two major issues affecting individuation
in the female: (1) the early relationship with the mother;
and (2) the girl's anatomy and its relationship to her psychic experience.

Psychoanalysis records the extraordinary role the
mother plays during the child's early infancy in the formation of the self-image. In a kind of mirroring, the infant
internalizes the image of itself as it is reflected to the child
in the mother's face and in her treatment of the child.[6]

Because of this process, the mother's conscious and
unconscious attitudes play a critical role in the girl's experience of herself. Some women do not value a daughter as
they would a son. Other women are not valued (by husbands, by culture at large) if they produce daughters and
not sons. Still others see *themselves* as devalued and hence
can only see their own products (children) as devalued.
Whatever the causal factors may be in forming the mother's
attitudes, those attitudes powerfully affect the infant girl's
sense of self-worth. But, although the mother's attitudes
influence much of the content of the child's self-image, I
don't think that this factor alone accounts for the girl's
difficulty in achieving autonomy so often noted both as a
cultural phenomena and a clinical symptom.

I think there is a factor that transcends the particular
contents of each individual mother's personal values. *All
mothers share one common experience: the mother sees herself in the
body of her infant daughter.* She relates to her daughter truly
narcissistically. The body the mother sees is known and
familiar, one with which she can have total identification;
one in which she recognizes her own past and present self.
In contrast, the boy can only be experienced by the mother

as different from herself. There cannot be the deep biological understanding of the male body experience that the mother has with her daughter. We have been accustomed in psychoanalysis to considering the boy as the narcissistic completion of the mother. Although he may be her treasure and prize, his body cannot be something with which she identifies in the same way as she does with the girl's body.[7]

It is, I think, self-evident that sameness facilitates sameness and difference facilitates difference. The mother's experience is reflected in the child who in turn experiences itself as "the same as" or "different from" the mother. The boy experienced as "different from" mother is aided in his path toward individuation in a way not available to the girl. The very structures of the relationships differ.

The contents of the parental expectation resulting from gender assignment further support individuation in the boy and oppose it in the girl. From the moment of gender assignment at birth, the mother expects that the boy will leave her, leave home, and have a career. In the toys given children and in the games played with them, these conscious and unconscious expectations are communicated. The subtle disapproval toward the boy in his nurturance play pushes him from this exercise of the early, automatic identifications with the mother; the encouragement of these activities reinforces this primary identification in the girl.

It has been suggested that the girl has an easier time in establishing and maintaining gender identity,[8] but gender identity, although central, is only one aspect of an identity synthesis. The very factor of her likeness to mother that makes it easier for her to maintain gender identity may stand in the way of other, equally important aspects of identity formation.

The second major factor, I think, that plays a role in

interfering with the girl's individuation lies in her own body. We are accustomed to saying that the ego is at core a body ego,[9] but we have generally omitted noting that the body ego includes sexual components. I believe this omission to be the heritage of earlier psychoanalytic theory that hypothesized identical prephallic phases for children of both sexes and omitted the role that sexual differences play in early ego formation and early identity formation. Freud ascribed the observed differences in male and female character to the psychological consequences of the girl's perception that she "lacks" a penis (and all that is implied in terms of castration anxiety or lack of castration anxiety). In early theory, the girl is a "boy" first and "becomes" a girl following the phallic phase. My thesis is that these observed differences reflect different physiological and psychological experiences during an earlier phase, during separation-individuation.

An early genital phase occurring during the separation-individuation phase has been observed. Once the early genital phase is experienced, it becomes part of the developing child's apparatus for discharge and becomes activated whenever there is stimuli requiring discharge.[10] If we consider the difference in the nature of the female and male sexual experience, they seem to suggest some of the observed differences in male and female functioning.[11]

More specifically, I believe these differences have ramifications for problems of individuation. The female sexual experience is a more internal, diffuse, generalized sensation than in the male. Being internal and unseen, it cannot be given a specific physical boundary. In contrast, the male genital experience is specific, local, and focused; the penis can be seen and felt, both tactilely and sensorily. One can act with it and on it. I propose that this kind of different bodily experience serves the individuating boy in a way not available to the girl in the midst of the same psychic development. I am suggesting that the diffuse, internalized, non-specific nature of the girl's early *sexual* experience is similar to the nonspecific, generalized, undifferentiated *psychic* experience during her early infancy. The boy's sexual experience, with its boundaried specificity, opposes the undifferentiated symbiotic experience and aids in building psychic boundaries from the inside (i.e., within the body experience). In addition, the penis is eminently suited for individuation, because it serves a natural anatomic vehicle for the drive outward, whereas the girl's excitement leads her inward and back to an earlier psychic state of boundary-lessness.

I think this role of the penis is reflected in clinical material. If we listen to women in relation to men, we hear, "Men can travel," "Men can go out in the world," "Men can be independent." What they are really saying is, "Men can go, they can leave." To put these statements into psychoanalytic language relevant to identity formation, what they are saying is that men can separate (individuate) and become separate human beings.

Here, then, is where I would place the famous (or infamous) "Anatomy is destiny."[12] *The mother's perception of the girl's anatomy and the power of gender assignment together with the girl's own early diffuse genital experience oppose individuation.* The blurred boundary between self and mother in early infancy is reflected and reinforced by her anatomy. There is a convergence of the girl child's experience in the outer world (first with her mother, then with cultural pressures) and in the inner world (within her own body).

Psychoanalysis has been attacked for the phallocentricity of its theory. It is, however, only a reflection of wide cultural values shared in almost every known culture. Many reasons have been offered to explain the veneration of the male. The issue of psychic individuation, separation from the omnipotent-seeming mother of early infancy, seems to provide a universal sphere of reference. *The function of the penis as an aid in individuation may well be a psychobiological origin of universal phallocentricity.*

Given the identical gender identity with the mother and the contribution of perception and sensory experience in the sexual sphere, together with culturally determined expectations and pressures, the girl has a more difficult time and fewer supports than the male in the individuation process.

2. ASPECTS OF SUPEREGO DEVELOPMENT THAT INTERFERE WITH AUTONOMY

Aspects of the female supergo contribute to the difficulties women have in achieving an identity synthesis that is adaptive to the cultural scene. Difficulties arise from both the nature of the superego's structure and the contents. There has been confusion between the superego as a structure and the contents of that structure.[13] "Structure" is an organization of prohibitions and admonitions to control and regulate drives as they are expressed in behavior and character. "Content" is the specific admonitions and prohibitions, the do's and don'ts. The superego's strength is not determined by the nature of its content, but by how powerfully the structure enforces that content. For example, the superego directive (content) to "be pliant" can create a "pliant" person who appears to have a weak superego but, in fact, it may take a very strong superego structure to enforce the directive.

Many of the observed differences between male and female superego are accounted for by the different contents. All of us who work with women know that the superego of women is not weaker than that of man; indeed, it is often tyrannical. Its contents contain character directives to be pliant, be flexible, be obedient, be pleasing, be

attentive, and to do as others expect you to do. The prohibitions are do not be aggressive, do not be assertive, autonomous, or independent. These latter qualities, forbidden
to women by a superego that declares that these traits are
unfeminine when exercised in pursuit of personal interests,
are permitted when they are exercised in the service of
other's needs (children, husband, home). Women are expected to be "in attendance." The cultural role may well be
a reflection of anatomy in that the woman's body is nurturing, supporting, and feeding. There may be a fitting
between the anatomic experience and the cultural expectation. However adaptive this attending model may be for a
woman in her nurturing role, it is maladaptive for many of
her new aspirations and needs.

Clinically, we repeatedly note that the slightest erup-
tion of aggression or self-assertion causes some women
great anxiety. Women in analysis, when confronted by an
emerging drive derivative, be it sexual or aggressive, will
anxiously ask, "What am I supposed to do . . .?" far more
frequently than men, who seem better able to enjoy aggressive and sexual fantasies. Women rarely can elaborate fantasies connected to these drives: "I want to . . .," "I feel like
doing . . .," "I see myself as. . . ." The assertive *I* brings
forth the anxiety because of the powerful superego commandment against such self-assertion. The impulse (aggression, sexuality) would be acceptable if someone (e.g.,
the analyst) would give permission for its expression. The
superego command to "follow" explains Freud's observation that women often change their standards to conform
with those of their lovers. I believe it also largely explains
the success of assertiveness training groups, as it is inherent in the title, that to be assertive is acceptable and desirable. In psychoanalytic terms, these groups have taken over
a superego function,[14] and are providing new content,
"thou shalt be assertive," in place of the old prohibition.
The ideals of the new external group (assertiveness train-

ing group) replace the ideals of the old internal group (parents, early cultural influences).

In considering the contents of the female superego one hears a repetition of the conflicts reviewed in the discussion of the separation-individuation process. Whereas the task of separation-individuation is the achievement of autonomy and independence, the contents of the superego for the girl contain directives against full achievement of autonomy. Once again, at this later stage of development, the girl may be pushed back toward the early infantile dependency.

At each stage of development, earlier structures and identifications related to the new ones are revived and influence the new stage of development.[15] This means that when a little girl's superego is being formed, her early relationship with her idealized mother plays a role. The mother of early childhood is identified with maternal, serving, nurturing qualities because she was totally nurturing to the infant girl and at the beck and call of the infant's needs. This image of the totally nurturing mother (in the experience of the infant who sees the mother only insofar as she serves its needs) is reawakened in terms of what the budding woman *should* be. This infantile image of the all-giving mother, a Mother Earth, is the basis of the ideal mother. Always a distortion resulting from the infant's immature perception, it nevertheless becomes the model for Mother and puts totally unrealistic pressures on women (from inside themselves as well as outside) to conform to this image. This idealized mother of infancy provides the contents of the superego commandments. This explains, I believe, the guilt so frequently encountered in working women when they are not in attendance on their family's needs. I have found intense guilt in women, whether or not they are really neglecting their families; indeed, women tend to feel guilty about the *wish* to work. This resurrected idealized image of what a mother "ought" to be makes a decision very difficult when a woman is faced with a conflict between pursuing her own career interests and the needs or wishes of her family. This idealized image of the good mother is reflected back to the woman in terms of cultural expectation. From the time she is a toddler, the cultural and parental ideal for the girl is that she be soft, pliant, and in attendance on others (i.e., her husband, her children, her parents).

Not only does the revived image of the idealized mother of infancy play a role in the content of the superego commandment for the girl, but the revived relationship also affects the structure. The resurrection of this early relationship also brings a revivial of the child's earlier mental state. That early mental state is characterized by confusion; the mother seems all-powerful. These factors affect the formation of the superego. As she was once totally helpless in relation to the omnipotent mother (in her perception), she feels helpless in relation to the superego. As she was once confused in her understanding of the mother's expectations, she feels confused in relation to the superego's commandments.

The idealized mother of early infancy is resurrected for the boy as well as for the girl. His superego commands him to be all-providing, all-protective, and all-powerful. Men are subject to much anxiety and despair when they do not live up to these internal (and external) expectations. Men perceive these male, paternal qualities as being like the powerful fathers of their childhood. But behind the powerful image of the father, one can recognize the mother of the nursery: providing, protecting, and seemingly all-powerful. That image of the mother is distant from the boy's ideal; it is remote, alien, and powerfully defended against. The intervening experiences for the male have transformed this early figure from the mother to the father.

As discussed in the section on separation-individuation, there has been a constant pressure on the boy to disidentify himself from the mother since early infancy. He is encouraged to protect and shelter in ways that are removed from the direct bodily nurturance. The direct expression of these wishes can lead the little boy into the most mortifying ridicule. The impulse to be nurturing may be the same as in the girl, but the form of expression must be quite different. His superego contents are, "Do not be like mother; be like father." Men do not face conflict over working as women do; they are confronted with guilt if they do not work. They seem to have little conflict about time and energy invested in careers, even when little time is left for their families; their work is not in conflict with the ideal images of themselves as fathers.

Freud described the superego in women: "Their superego is never so inexorable, so impersonal, so independent of its emotional origins as we require it to be in men."[16] These differences have been ascribed to the absence of castration anxiety in the girl. I think, however, that one might reformulate the source of the differences in terms of the resurrected omnipotent ideal mother of infancy and its effects on both content and structure of the superego. The girl is not so independent of her emotional origins; she is much closer to the early dependency and accompanying mental state. Because of differences throughout the boy's development (particularly separation-individuation), including the transformation of the idealized, grandiose image from the mother to the father, the boy is less susceptible to these early influences. The resulting superego in the boy *is* more distant and impersonal. Although the girl's superego is different, it is not weak. It is quite powerful, in the image of the grandiose mother of infancy. Because of the revived early state, it has the capacity to be less rigid; it is not weak, but rather it is flexible.

To reiterate, at the stage of superego development, both the boy and girl are subject to the resurrected idealized image of the mother and the early mental states that characterized that period. Because of the differences in development, the boy is not as susceptible to these influences encompassing nurturing aspects and the ego diffusion that accompany the early stages. The boy is more resistive to regressive influences, while the girl has no place to go but back. The revival of the earlier states gives the female superego a different characteristic than that of the male; it has the capacity for greater flexibility. The female superego is not weak, either structurally or in terms of contents. However, because of its different structure and contents, it does oppose the aims of autonomy and assertiveness that women are trying to attain.

3. Problems in Forming Adaptive Identifications

Analytic literature has, for several decades, been preoccupied with the role of the mother in the child's development. The father, central to most of the theories of Freud and his contemporaries, appears to have faded from his once critical role. Analyses of women have mostly been directed at analyzing the conflicts, rivalries, and rages that have interfered with the girl's "proper" identification with her mother. Analyses of women's relations to their fathers have been aimed at resolving those envies and conflicts toward men that have kept them from having "feminine" lives.

But inasmuch as today's young woman needs to go beyond this aim, the traditional suppression of "masculinity" in the girl's character is maladaptive, and the father must be considered not only as an erotic object, but as an object of identification and ego resource. Psychoanalysis has not addressed itself sufficiently to this aspect of the role of the father.

As the girl identifies with her father and he emerges as

an ego resource, considerable anxiety is aroused in both parents. There are in operation massive cultural prohibitions against individuals behaving in ways that differ from the sex role models. I call these prohibitions "forbidden identifications." The girl who wishes to identify with aspects of her father must deal with anxiety and conflict in relation to both parents and society, and within herself.

Considerable conflict may arise between mother and daughter if the daughter wishes to break with familiar female roles and develop a career. The threat to the mother is twofold. First, she must "lose" her daughter; when the girl goes off into the career world, she leaves home, physically and emotionally. When girls remained at home, they were safe from the conflicts over separation; so were their mothers. Neither mother nor daughter had to face the pain and loss of leaving.

> "You have a son 'till he gets a wife;
> You have a daughter all your life."

When the daughter chooses a career, she is interrupting the generational repetition of women in the home; the mother-daughter tie perpetuated by the daughter's continuing the mother's role is broken.

Second, the mother's entire character structure as described earlier is threatened. Her repressions of autonomy, aggression, and aspirations for success in the outer world are threatened by the daughter who refused to relinquish these aspects of herself. The stimulation of these long-quieted feelings in the mother causes her considerable agitation and anxiety as the defensive structure is threatened.

Patients have described their mother's reactions to their career aspirations: "Mother ignored me as if I hadn't spoken"; "She seemed to feel betrayed"; "They always worried about what my brothers would do when they grew up, never about us girls"; "I don't think my mother ever 'saw' me"; or "I never came into focus." Such statements often include boundary references either implicitly or explicitly. Issues of being seen, heard, and focused all imply an identity reference. Women who have surrendered their own autonomy and independence in obedience to personal and cultural ideals cannot tolerate the expression of these affects in their daughters. For daughters who wish to have for themselves some of the "masculine" qualities, the traditional balance (through projection and unconscious identification) is upset. Women who have surrendered their autonomy in order to "be women" are threatened by ERA as much as men are. Their ego boundaries have had to exclude autonomy in order to achieve inner grace with their mothers and their fathers; they cannot welcome it in their daughters.

In forming critical identifications a mother-daughter conflict arises from within the daughter herself. When the girl is in the oedipal phase and later when she is in adolescence, she has the task of forming *appropriate* identifications with her mother. Residues of the symbiotic phase are revived, as mentioned in the discussion of superego formation, and they complicate these identifications. When we hear of perpetual storms between mother and daughter during these stages, I think we are seeing a constant exercise of the NO muscle. Spitz[17] described the toddler's NO as containing an individuating statement, "No, I am not you, or like you"; here the child is aspiring toward autonomy. The girl, during the oedipal and adolescent stages, is struggling simultaneously to attain or retain individuation (be different) at the same time that she is forming identifications with her mother to consolidate her femininity. She is caught in tremendous conflict, trying simultaneously to be *unlike* (retain autonomy) and to be *like* her mother (retain femininity).

This conflict accounts for many of the endless mother-

daughter battles in childhood and adolescence. The familiar interpretation of these battles as being the result of
competition for the father is yet another expression of analytic phallocentricity.

If the girl is able to use the father as an ego resource
and identify with his ability to leave mother, the intensity
of much of the girl's struggle would be relieved. Many
fathers do not seem able to do for their daughters what they
do so readily for their sons (i.e., offer an alliance, a friend-
ship, an identification model).

Daughters who turn to their fathers as an ego resource
frequently arouse deep anxiety in them. Men's protection
of masculine territory from women is a well-known cultural
phenomena reflected in men's schools, clubs, and bars.
This need to keep women out is a reflection of the male's
need to protect his boundaries (separation-individuation).
When this need to keep women out and away extends to the
daughter who has a wish or need to identify with his ability
to leave (separate from) the mother or to succeed in the
outer world, it leaves the girl child without supports for her
aspirations. Recent documentation of the role of mentors[18]
for successful women demonstrates how women have
found this identification figure in the world when their
fathers have not provided it.[19]

Lax[20] describes several cases in which fathers permitted their daughters to identify with them professionally
while still depreciating femininity as a whole and their
mothers in particular. These fathers made their daughters
"exceptions" by encouraging them in professional spheres
while simultaneously devaluing women as love objects. As
a result, these women, whose histories Lax traced, were in
constant conflict. They could not identify with their "devalued" mothers; at the same time, identifications with their
fathers could only be made at the cost of their femininity.
They were split in their sexual, professional, and maternal
lives. They were able to find little gratification, even se-

quentially, but remained in constant conflict, unable to find peace either as wives, mothers, or at work. In other words, these women were unable to achieve an adaptive identity synthesis.

In discussing separation-individuation problems, I discussed the different sexual experiences in the boy and girl. The boy often relies on the anatomical difference to establish individuation. In essence, he says "I am not one with the nurturing mother. See, I am different." The more the male defines and defends his individuation and his maleness based on the different sexual anatomy, the less likely he is to open his ego boundaries and welcome identifications by his daughter. It is not the penis itself (castration anxiety), but the penis as proof of individuation, that must be guarded and protected. Or, it is not the penis, but *individuation,* which is being protected by use of the penis.

Cultural and analytic phallocentricity is quite profound. Phallocentric men and women are unable to see the vagina as an active organ. They see only the penis as active. Why is there this almost universal insistence that the female lacks an "executive organ"[21] and that only the penis is active?

It has been proposed that insistence on the phallus as powerful is necessary to both sexes to overcome being helpless at the hands of the once all-powerful mother.[22] Not only was the mother powerful in the infantile psychic experience, but in traditional homes with the father absent at work, the mother wielded great power in the day-to-day routines of life. The powerlessness of the developing child is quite total; the father becomes a symbol of strength and power over the mother. He leaves the mother; he has sexual power over her. In other words, phallocentricity ensures that someone is stronger than mother, who was once stronger than everybody. The penis, then, gives assurance that such power does exist in the world and that those who possess the penis have that power. As the mother needs to be overpowered to ensure against psychic helplessness, the vagina as a symbol of the powerful mother must also be denied its activity. As the omnipotent psychic mother threatens psychic reengulfment, the vagina becomes the symbol of physical reengulfment. Thus both men and women must preserve "men's prerogatives" as a vehicle of power to reverse the powerlessness of early infancy. The girl who wishes to identify with her father challenges this function, and, hence, there is a culturally forbidden identification of the girl with her father.

In addition to coping with forbidden identifications, girls themselves find it difficult to identify with their fathers. The most obvious difficulty stems from biological differences; in the same way that mother responds to the like and unlike qualities of her infants, so does the developing girl feel unlike her father.

I have found that a welcoming paternal attitude either from the father or a significant male figure, such as a mentor, or perhaps later in the analytic transference situation, has facilitated the critical identifications. Fathers, mentors, and analysts can recognize and welcome the girl's interests and activities and provide an ego resource. *It is important that this movement toward the significant male not be misinterpreted as erotic.*

The synthesizing of critical identifications with both mother and father is a difficult task; it requires the girl to be flexibly in touch with different aspects of herself. To be feminine and yet assertive, to work and yet be able to nurture requires a great deal of libido and strength and flexibility to fulfill both roles adequately.

Psychoanalytically, we must be cognizant of forbidden identifications operating from parents and society toward the girl child. We have from the mother, out of her competitiveness, "Do not be like me" and, out of the protection of her image of femininity, "Don't be like your father" and "Don't leave me." From the father we have the classical depreciating attitude toward women that makes it hard for the girl to be like mother but, simultaneously, we have from the father "Do not be like me" (stay out of my territory). I think attention to these conflicting identifications and the facilitating trasferential environment in which the female can successfully identify with both parents and be feminine and yet find the gratification available in the world is something to which analysts must be attuned. In a way we must be the carriers of the facilitating identifications for the woman to achieve a rewarding, fulfilling, and yet feminine identity synthesis.

Chapter 6

WOMEN'S CHOICE OF A DUAL ROLE: BRIEF NOTES ON A DEVELOPMENTAL DETERMINANT[1]

Charlotte Kahn, Ed.D.

THE PROBLEM

Alerted by the communications of activists and the counterarguments of the defenders of the traditional role of women, a personal incident brought to my attention the complicated, sometimes difficult, and yet satisfying circumstances of the women who function both as professionals and homemakers.

> Some months ago, a friend sent me a copy of an article. Attached was a brief personal note that read: "Richard is fine; the children are busy at school, and I even have had time to go to the library."
>
> In one sentence, my friend had revealed her characteristic concerns. In a single, brief statement, she had mentioned two equally important aspects of her life: homemaker and professional. Subsequently, during a discussion, she indicated that she desires to be, and enjoys her roles as, understanding mother, enthusiastic sexual partner, above-average cook, and capable teacher. Furthermore, she appreciates the opportunity to expand her ideas and formulate them for publication.
>
> We agree that she could have relinquished neither role without doing violence to her personality, without detriment to her performance in the remaining role, and without disturbance to her relationships with husband, children, and friends.
>
> Is she a driven woman? Competitive? Greedy? Is she dissatisfied? Expressing penis envy? Fear of death?

Attention to women's place in modern society often has focused on the hardships of women who have adopted a role assigned to them by the culture and dictated by the needs of other members of their society. Many women have confessed to feeling guilty about the time, thought, and energy spent in some fashion unrelated to their children. They have felt ashamed of their so-called neurotic dissatisfaction with the mother role. Wives have admitted to limiting their efforts in order to avoid surpassing their

husbands' achievements, especially their husbands' earning power. Recently, in apparent desperation, some wives
have left their husbands; some mothers have abandoned
their children.

Unnoticed has been the small number of women who,
long before the emergence of the most recent women's
liberation movement, have struggled as individuals to
maintain a way of life suited to their temperament, albeit
contrary to the customary ways of society.

In the past, spinsterhood was an alternative for those
women who were not temperamentally inclined to adopt
the culturally assigned role. Unhappy conditions such as
widowhood, a husband's illness, or the desire for material
possessions beyond the husband's means also justified
work outside the home. More frequently, women and their
male partners happily rationalized that it was all right for
the wife to work as long as she was not required to function
as a full-time mother (i.e., before childbirth and after the
children were sufficiently grown). "After the children were
sufficiently grown" has been interpreted variously as entrance into first grade, high school, or leaving home. As late
as 1970, in a predominantly lower-middle-class college
group, only the very few young women whose mothers had
chosen to work could entertain the possibility of doing so
themselves. Even they envisioned almost insurmountable
obstacles since, for the representatives of this social class,
hiring child-care personnel was an altogether foreign and
unacceptable practice. Most often their mothers had
managed with the help of grandmothers.

But who are the individuals who, without relinquishing
their privileges of marital partnership and regardless of
economic need, chose to pursue a career at a time when it
was unfashionable? What motivated them?

Several emotionally or physically unwell women of our
acquaintance improved without therapy when they became

seriously involved in full- or part-time monetarily rewarding responsibilities outside the home. Their marital relationships improved in that, in accordance with their
husbands' expectations, they more readily accepted the
submissive role at home. Their experiences seem to resemble Helene Deutsch's findings that "... many women who
preserve the activity of their egos, and use it for sublimation purposes, are extremely passive and masochistic in
their sexual behavior."[2]

In spite of these observations, it seems unlikely that all
nonconforming women—either those who chose work in
the past or those who will choose homemaking careers in
the society of the future—are doing so for neurotic reasons.
Acceptance or rejection of prevailing societal attitudes
does not explain adequately why, in the same society, some
women who are discontented become happier in themselves and in their family life when they embark on a career
while others anticipate family discontent as a result of professional activities, despite a promise of improved financial
conditions. Subtle distinguishing factors must be at work.

Perhaps variations in the early life experiences of
women determine their expectations and aims. For example, are the differing role choices of women determined by
differing identifications during the formative years? Did the
women who chose the dual role model themselves during
childhood after an admired working woman? In an initial
attempt to answer these questions, a very informal pilot
study was planned.

THE PROCEDURE

The investigator resolved to interview each woman who
was known or became known to her during the first half of
1973 and who, as wife and mother, continued her career
without interruption. The 12 women, whose experiences

led to the following conclusions, are all university gradu-
ates; many have advanced degrees. One factory worker was
brought to our attention. She lives in the Midwest, could
not be interviewed and, therefore, was not included here.
However, it is of some interest that her sister's report in-
dicated that for the factory worker no financial need to
work exists, that the structure and relationships of the family of origin resemble those of the 12 professional women
in the most significant respects, and that there appears to
be a strong inner need to combine outside work with family
life. The small sample of women interviewed includes an
analysand of the investigator, some of her colleagues,
friends, neighbors, and friends of friends.

As a result of the informality of the procedure, the
nature and amount of material gathered in each case is
varied. For example, much more is known about the
teacher, who has had many years of analysis, than about the
young social worker from the farm, who is not very intro-
spective and who was seen only once.

The conduct of the interviews was semistructured;
open-ended questions were posed, followed by more direct
questions whenever necessary to complete the desired information. The setting of the interviews was intentionally
very informal and relaxed. For example, in several in-
stances, the writer arranged a luncheon meeting with an
acquaintance or with a colleague. In the course of general
or professional conversation, the investigator mentioned
her curiosity about the circumstances that might have contributed to the other woman's decision to embark on a
career and to continue her work even after the arrival of
children. Twice, an acquaintance who had been interviewed became sufficiently interested in the topic to ar-
range a dinner party for the express purpose of introducing
the investigator to other subjects and their spouses. With
only a single exception, the conversation during these interviews was animated, free-flowing, and spontaneously re-

ferred to various members of the family of origin. When mothers or grandmothers were not specifically mentioned as working or career women, the investigator asked about them. Only after several interviews had been conducted did it become apparent that the father's attitude toward his daughter might be an important factor in a woman's choice of a dual role. At that point, questions regarding the father-daughter relationship were regularly included in the interviews. In order to gather the requisite information from women interviewed prior to this point, they were reinterviewed, with the exception of one social worker and an editor. However, since then, several other women have been casually questioned, always with concurring results (to be discussed below).

As a result of the informality of the investigative method, data indirectly related to the topic of this paper became available (i.e., while the husbands of personal acquaintances and neighbors were already known to me, during the dinner parties the husbands and wives could be observed together, at least in limited interaction). Of course, several questions arose. Do the husbands of career women share common features of personality such as relatively high tendency to submission? Are they weak, passive men? Or are they especially strong and supportive? How do they view their lives in contrast to men married to homemakers? One husband declared that he has better conversations with his wife than he could have if she were not stimulated through her professional activities. In this particular situation, husband and wife are in different branches of the same profession. The husband stressed the binding aspects of the shared profession; however, there are some indications that strong competitive currents also prevail. One of the women interviewed thought that her husband "married his father." An exploration of the meaning of this remark revealed her respect for her husband's strengths and successes, a recognition of his weaknesses, and acute

A change for the better...

From time to time we introduce a change...and when we do, it's important to us that you are aware of it. As you may have noticed, there is a slight difference on the face of your documents—the area in which the dollar amount is written numerically has been framed by a shaded box.

Research has shown that defining such an area tends to improve legibility. That means more efficient handling of documents. And the more accurate and rapid the handling, the better you can be served. When it comes to change, that's the best reason we know.

APPROVE THESE DOCUMENTS
You are the final inspector!

Every effort has been made to assure accuracy in the printing of your order, though an error could occur.

PLEASE EXAMINE THE FOLLOWING:

1. Your Name
2. Name Of Your Financial Institution (branch when printed)
3. Your Account Number (when printed).

IF YOU FIND AN ERROR, NOTIFY YOUR FINANCIAL INSTITUTION IMMEDIATELY!
All orders are furnished on the condition that liability is limited to the replacement of the incorrectly printed order.

Protect Your Account

- Never use pencil or erasable ink pen on these documents.

- Keep these documents in a safe place. If they are lost or stolen, notify your financial institution immediately.

- Destroy unused documents.

- Use your documents in sequential order and reconcile your statement promptly. If you find a discrepancy, notify your financial institution.

SEE REVERSE SIDE

sensitivity to his motivations, as well as a recognition of her own forcefulness and of the complementary character of their marital interaction.

Also related to the informality of the study was the opportunity to learn about some of the subsequent events in these women's lives, which were directly related to their choice of a dual role. For example, in three cases, the women relocated when their husbands were transferred by their companies. In two cases, the choice (whether to relocate or to remain in the New York area) was a very difficult one, because the women's career opportunities in the new locations were seemingly nonexistent or nebulous at the moment the decision had to be made. Fortunately, the women's competence and perseverance, laced with a little luck, produced a satisfactory position. Indeed, the engineer found a job superior to the one she had left.

Great changes have occurred during the 3 years that have elapsed since the data for this article were gathered. Not only are an increasing number of young women choosing the dual role, but a significant number of families are experiencing "creative separations." During the last 2 months, I have met or heard about six women who leave their husbands and children for half of each week to pursue their careers in locations too far removed for commuting, two men whose wives are continuing their careers in the original location while the husbands live away from home 4 days weekly, and one man who has relocated in order to follow his wife, who was offered an interesting job far away from their former domicile.

THE WOMEN

Two of the interviews conducted at the outset of the project were meager in content. Nevertheless, they pointed encouragingly toward confirmation of the original hunch that identifications during the formative years affect a woman's choice of role in adulthood.

A young, pregnant social worker (A) described life on the farm in a three-generational family setting. Not very much was said about the father except that he went out to work as any man would be expected to do. Grandfather and grandmother fully cooperated in the running of the farm; in fact, grandmother performed some of the chores not ordinarily done by American farm women, such as turning the hay in the field. Mother taught at the local school until her second child was born, when she began tutoring at home. In short, the young woman, about to embark on her own career in private practice after a few years of employment, seemed to be following in her mother's footsteps. Furthermore, given the model of her grandmother, it appeared to be no accident that her plans for private practice included some collaboration and cross-referral with her husband, who was engaged in a related profession.

Other indications that early identifications help determine the choices of the dual role came from a middle-aged editor (B) who spoke admiringly of her aunt, an active working woman, worldly wise and charming, and from two sisters (C and D), an engineer and a psychiatrist, whose mother had studied law and whose grandmother had worked in the family business.

One psychoanalyst (E) gave a partial family history that included four generations of women. According to her, there was never a doubt in her mind, as far back as she can consciously remember, that one day she would be a person doing important work. She wanted to go to school and played school with slightly older children long before she was of school age. An older cousin brought his primer, and she practiced writing the ABC's. In third grade she decided to attend the university.

At the same time, there was never a doubt that E would have babies. She knew that she would have babies before she knew "the facts of life." When she asked where babies came from (she thinks sometime between the ages of 2 and 4), she was told "the stork flies high in the sky, carrying the baby in a diaper which he holds in his beak; then he lands on the balcony to deliver the baby." She knew then that she still did not know the truth about babies. She did not believe the stork story.

This psychoanalyst's mother was indisputably subservient to her father. Mother pursued her work avocationally, partly as a result of personal inhibitions and partly in deference to her husband, who insisted on being the sole provider for the family. The mother's submission to the father was rationalized as tact, diplomacy, fostering peace in the family, and, generally, as an acceptable demeanor in relation to the "man of the house." On the contrary, as a young girl and especially as a teenager, E considered her mother's stance to be unacceptable. Instead, she preferred what she experienced with and heard about her grandmothers. Her maternal grandmother had inherited her own father's business, which she managed throughout most of her life with the help of her husband and consort. After his death, she carried on alone. E visited often. From the age of 5 on, E participated in the activities of the store, covering boxes, scribbling make-believe sales checks before she could write properly, acting in the Christmas pageant for the benefit of the employees. Her memory of her grandmother is of a forceful, sometimes pedantic personality—a gentlewoman in charge! She was a lady who was treated with respect during her active years and, later, pampered gladly when sick and frail.

How was it possible, E wondered as a teenager, that her mother could claim strength on the basis of patience and endurance vis-á-vis the father, when her grandmother had demonstrated real and apparent strength and readily discernible effectiveness? As a psychoanalyst, E had learned to understand that her mother's role probably always had been one of submission to the strong grandmother and, furthermore, that E's father replicated the grandmother's personality in many ways. In other words, the complementary relationship between grandmother and mother was repeated between mother and father. An additional factor explaining E's mother's personality was the personality of great-grandmother. Great-grandmother took major responsibility for the daily care of E's mother while grandmother worked. Great-grandmother was warm and caring to excess. She earned the nickname, Miss Jump-Up, so ready was she to serve and meet the needs of others.

E's paternal grandmother was 76 years old at the time of E's birth. E has visual memories of an old-fashioned looking woman sitting in her chair. The more meaningful, emotional memories were determined by the old woman's lively facial expressions, her active participation in conversations that E, as a tiny girl, did not understand. The paternal family lived in a small, semirural town. Visits there were exhilarating. There were geese, goats, chickens, horses, vegetable gardens, quaint houses, and cobblestone streets. And, adjoining the grandparents' house, a small store contained yardgoods of the most exciting colors and smooth, satiny textures. What a thrill to have her aunt cut a broad, gaudy ribbon to tie a bow in her hair, while happily reminiscing about years past when Grandmother was young and strong when she hurried into the store whenever the tinkle of the bell announced the arrival of a customer at the door! This was Grandmother's store—her very own. Grandfather had his separate business. Grandmother was strong, energetic, principled, and generous. She bore six children and raised five to be successful adults; she ran her store, tended her garden, and supervised her household. Paternal grandmother was a no-nonsense woman who knew her mind. Often, one of E's uncles admiringly commented that he saw his mother in his niece.

Here, then, are five women who seem to have chosen their roles on the basis of an identification with a working mother or grandmother or, in one case, an aunt. Yet not all of the interviews supported this proposition. Some showed a similarity to Lynn Schneider's results,[3] indicating a *tendency* in the direction of identification with the mother, but no *significant* relationship between identification with mother and orientation toward home or career. Four women who chose the dual role for themselves revealed in the course of the interview that their mothers were homemakers in the traditional fashion.

A mathematician (F) who resented her mother's dissatisfaction and complaints about the demands and restrictions of housekeeping. However, she saw her grandmother happily, though somewhat ritualistically, engaged in preparing and serving foods on special occasions.

A psychoanalyst (G) whose experience with her mother resembled that of the mathematician with hers. Her father took her along to work frequently; she remembers sitting under the counter in the small store.

A political scientist (H) whose fastidious mother could hardly tolerate anyone else in her kitchen.

A psychiatrist (I) whose mother happily embraced her role of homemaker. Mother was esteemed as a good cook and an excellent baker. Mother's major goal and greatest pleasure was to please her husband, who amply rewarded her with praise and protection. However, it often appeared to the children in this household that an air of condescension and mockery pervaded the praise, because the ultimate standards by which people were judged were rationality, emotional detachment, scientific objectivity. Mother's attitudes and behavior exemplified impulsiveness, emotional involvement, and personal bias. Clearly, mother was less educated than father, less intelligent, politically and socially naive. Her only hope for recognition was to be a dependable handmaiden to her husband, who would graciously let her share in his glory. She was allowed to stand by his side backstage as fans and fellows crowded around, hoping to shake hands or, with luck, to have the program autographed.

With a father intensely involved in a career and a mother desperately involved with father, both son and daughter felt themselves to be vaguely superfluous, sometimes neglected and rejected.

During the early adolescent years, she simultaneously rebelled and sought a place to belong, to be accepted. Turning away from parents who were involved with themselves, rejecting the rational, philosophical attitudes, she identified with a protégé of her father and converted to Catholicism. In her father's eyes she had sinned; she had let herself be drugged by "the opiate of the masses." Her passionate commitment to religion lasted only 3 years. When she emerged from the cocoon of the church, it was not to prepare herself to be a good wife. She enrolled in a demanding women's college in order to prepare for a career, and became enmeshed in affairs with men whom her family regarded with disdain. She ensured that she would not be cast in the role of her mother. She displayed a "negative identification" with her mother. She now is married to a man who is her equal socially, professionally, and in personal attractiveness. Her three children are integral links in her life with her husband.

Although from the point of view of these four women their mothers' homemaker roles were undesirable, the mothers themselves were not sufficiently unhappy to change their life patterns. One might speculate that in the eyes of the subjects of this study, the low status of a homemaker, or the demands and restrictions of that role, caused them to turn away from it. But does a woman working the farm endure fewer restrictions? Are days spent in the store less demanding? Do the pupils who come for tutoring require less patience from their teacher than children and husband? Why did daughters of working women not shy away from the hardships of a dual role? And if mothers or grandmothers provide models of undesirable roles, why do some women partially reject their model? What differentiated the women who chose dual roles from those who chose the unmarried life or homosexuality?

The comparison and contrasts in two additional cases seemed to offer a clue.

A psychologist (J) had a mother who worked part-time. Both mother and grandmother accepted the homemaker's role very matter of factly.

The psychologist, a very successful lecturer and author of several published articles, had no doubts about her aims. She steadfastly pursued her studies despite parental pressure to "settle down" and despite her husband's unsympathetic demands. For instance, while she was preparing an article for publication, he asked her with annoyance and impatience whether she couldn't do something useful. Couldn't she address the Christmas cards or wrap the packages? The psychologist is not guilt-ridden about "leaving" her three children during working hours. By all appearances, the children are happy and above-average individuals.

J apparently formed a positive identification with her grandmother as homemaker and with her mother in the dual role. She says about her mother, "She enjoyed working and regarded the world of work as an exciting arena for new experiences and new friends. However, in the family she had little power in making decisions, and my father was the dominant one. . . ."

On the contrary,

> A teacher (K), whose mother spent most of her time "in the store" and, instead of cooking, sent her children to eat out in a restaurant, is in an almost constant state of conflict regarding her responsibilities as homemaker and mother, in spite of the fact that, according to all reports, the children have received love and intelligent care.

K seems to have identified positively with her mother as a working woman while simultaneously establishing a negative identification with her mother as homemaker. As a child she felt uncomfortable with her caretakers and rejected by a mother whom she perceived as selfish and narcissistic. Under no circumstances does this teacher want to expose her children to similar experiences. Yet she feels compelled to go on as a professional woman—despite her own conflicts, despite her husband's indifference and frequent opposition.

DISCUSSION

J accepted, without resentment, both her mother's and grandmother's roles in life. K bears deep resentments to this very day. J had the opportunity to identify with grandmother, the homemaker. Instead, like mother, she chose the dual role. K had the opportunity to live out a negative identification with mother, the working woman; instead, she chose the dual role for herself. The element common to these women's life experiences was their relationship to their father. *Their father's influence became the fulcrum that balanced the values determining these women's choice of the dual role.*

Both women loved and respected their fathers. Both fathers were intelligent, interested, partially self-educated men who related to their daughters primarily in a verbal way, sharing ideas instead of solely admiring them for their good looks or their grace.

Further inquiry revealed that the relationship to the father was similar in all the cases under discussion where the information was available: that is, the relationship between father and daughter could be characterized as companionable and verbal, if not exclusively intellectual. Father's goals and expectations for the daughter were not founded as much on his appreciation of her feminine charms as on her abilities which, nevertheless, often included homemaking abilities. This was true of the sisters (engineer and psychiatrist, C and D) whose father had a reputation of being a "formidable man"; the mathematician who confided in her father during pleasant walks in the woods; and the two psychoanalysts, one of whom (G) spent much time in the company of her father sitting under the counter in the candy store, while the other (E) who—in addition to identifying with her two working grandmothers —occasionally joined her father when he visited clients and spent brief moments in his office scribbling on pads and admiring the "mammoth" safe. The psychiatrist (I) earned her father's silent admiration when she demonstrated intelligence as well as when she displayed her good looks.

In all these cases, it appears that when the girl turned to her father in order to earn his love, the particular *conditions of the father-daughter relationship were such that, in the course of their interaction, the young girl's ego expanded sufficiently to enable her to sacrifice a measure of dependency and submission.* With father's aid, often at his side while he pursued his occupation, she developed skills and mastery that helped her to resist the "inhibiting influence as regards both her aggression and her activity" that "the environment exerts," and that would "bring her back to her mother for . . . infantile love demands."[4]

Some confirmation of the importance of the father's role as a determinant of the daughter's choice of the dual role comes from two additional cases.

> L is a lawyer whose father expected men and women to collaborate in supporting the family. Her mother declared that she "wouldn't have been much use to him" had she not come to supervise the office while he was out buying. This father never questioned whether daughter would take up a career. He only asked her on which one she had decided!

> In the case of M, the father urged his daughter to prepare herself to earn her livelihood, because, he admitted, the possibility existed that she would not marry. Besides, he cautioned, one never knows when a depression or a wave of anti-Semitism will hit. M became a brilliant economist, college professor, and mother of two lively, precocious children.

Evidently, M's father could not openly contradict the then prevailing cultural attitudes regarding women's role. But however he rationalized his own attitudes, he did show an active interest in his wife's teaching career and strongly encouraged his daughter to fashion a career for herself.

Thus, the women in this sample were not bribed with love as a compensation for giving up aggression. Instead, they were rewarded by their fathers for their assertiveness. In addition, they could reap the pleasures of mastery and the satisfactions intrinsic to the activities they learned to pursue. Furthermore, the possibilities for sublimation offered them protection against the use of dependence as a shield against their hostile impulses.

Nevertheless, a variety of circumstances caused the women to doubt, yet to continue to strive for their mother's love and understanding. In some of these cases, the original disappointment with a narcissistic, less intelligent, sick, or absent mother, or mother's preoccupation with a younger sibling, seemed to cause the daughter to turn to her father somewhat prematurely. The yearning for the mother continued, but the passive position now seemed too insecure, too dangerous. Was it not safer to emulate the competent, active father, whom mother loves and respects? At the same time, positive identification with the mother or her surrogate remained important and was reinforced by the knowledge that, even in those cases where father implied or stated somewhat different expectations of his daughter, he had chosen her mother to be his wife. Consequently, in accordance with their temperamental needs, the women identified selectively with both father and mother, feeling relatively assured that one or both parents would, on some level, approve.

Undoubtedly, such a course of development is more complicated than one that represents the simple (stylized) version of identification with mother and love for father. Undeniably, the women interviewed for this project experienced, in addition to the sociocultural conflict, much intrapsychic conflict in the course of their development. Of all the women mentioned, K (the teacher) seems to have been most keenly aware of dissonance within herself.

> K. not only had to identify with both parents, not only to integrate two sets of values and to fuse them into a superego, she also had to contend with the split image of mother. K had to cope with a hated and an admired internalized image deriving from the same object—her mother.
>
> The same unforgiving attitude toward the mother, who preferred working in the store to preparing meals for the children, was directed toward herself when she became aware in herself of a wish to participate in nonfamily activities outside the home. Every such decision caused agony. Often, even when K had performed all the necessary tasks

at home in preparation for her absence, she rushed back as soon as possible. Lingering with colleagues and friends caused her to hate herself on her children's behalf, as she had resented the mother who, after a workweek in the store, stepped out with the father on Sundays. On the other hand, K's mother did provide: she, not K's father, was the life of the business. She dressed her girls attractively and was, herself, always fashionably attired. K was proud of her beautiful mother. In these matters, K has emulated her mother; she still buys clothes for her adult daughters and is fastidious about her own makeup and attire.

Therefore, the conflict is centered around the ambivalence over the mother who simultaneously achieved for and abandoned her children. The abandoning mother became the object of negative identification and the bad internalized image; the achieving mother became the object of positive identification and the good internalized image. Father, on the other hand, represented ethical ideals in theoretical formulation, displayed consistent principled behavior, and was involved in social action. K experiences some feeling of awe vis-á-vis the image of her father; she used to experience some fear of his raging temper. However, K does not consider these seemingly opposite characteristics as dissonant or conflicting. Instead, the passion that fired father's ethical-social principles and actions is the same passion that occasionally manifested itself in his angry disapproval. K has identified positively with these paternal characteristics, so much so that she is repeatedly surprised when confronted by unprincipled, shady, selfish behavior. Similarly, she has only recently recognized that others do not accept her in her self-appointed position of standard-bearer and upholder of principles and that they do not understand the annoyance, impatience, and anger that K thinks is a most natural expression of disapproval of less-than-ideal behavior.

It seems important to emphasize that K's problems center around the identification with mother, the object of ambivalence. It is the fear of becoming like the abandoning mother that tinges the negative identification, the nurturing wife-mother-homemaker, with some rigidity resembling a compulsion. The problem does not seem to arise from the selective identification with mother and father. The achieving mother and the philosophical father live together harmoniously in K. They are synthesized in her work life.

Indeed, K's attempt at resolution of her conflict, her integration of maternal and paternal ideals, created a complex fabric of superego content and produced a wide range of skills. And the same can be said of the other women who were interviewed. Exciting individuals leading productive lives, they did not show symptoms of the masculinity complex, the ". . . predominance of active and aggressive tendencies that lead to conflict with the woman's environment and above all with the remaining feminine world;"[5] nor did they show an exaggerated submissiveness and overt dependence on a husband who replaces the real or longed-for mother. Instead, their personalities represented a synthesis of mother and father images and of their respective ideals. As a result of the fusion of identifications, in contrast to a substitution or giving up of impulses, these women seem able to "subordinate their emotions" to ideals without completely sacrificing "warm emotions" for their husbands and children.[6] Indeed, the unresolved remnants of their relationship to their mothers, reinforced by the partial identification with the active mother or surrogate, enable them to treat their children with the warmth and understanding they once wished for themselves. Furthermore, they generally seek and seem able to accept a degree of nurturance from their husbands, even while sharing a "common devotion to something impersonal."[7] Helene Deutsch implies that such devotion takes the place of and is less desirable than the direct expression of what she calls "warm emotion." Marie Curie is the example par excellence that both are possible in the same relationship. And in her case, one can see clearly the identification with the loving illness-restricted mother, the image of mother as a professional woman, and the father's expressions of love and concern for the children through intellectual activities.

In two of the above cases, some disturbances are known to exist as a result of a continuing defensive striving for omnipotence on the part of the woman. This striving, which is in conflict with her passive needs and serves as a defense against feelings of infantile helplessness, might well have been a major contributing motivation for the dual identification. In those cases where the disappointment in the mother and the resulting experience of vulnerability were great, one might expect not only a turning toward the father, but an effort on the part of the child to take care of herself on all fronts by becoming like (indeed, better than) father *and* mother. However, when the mother has been forgiven, when the conflict has been resolved, the defensive aspects of the dual identification can yield to sublimation.[8] In the case of the teacher, the conflict had not been resolved at the time of her marriage, and she chose a partner who resembles her mother and repeats her mother's failings: his love for her is narcissistic. Consequently, she feels misunderstood and unsupported. Until recently, she continued to try to defend her vulnerability by strengthening her armor of knowledge, skills, and performance. Her striving for competence is seen as a striving for power and protection and also as a way to increased self-esteem. Most important is the memory of her father as an intellectual whose love and respect could be earned by achieving academically. At this point in her analysis, she is beginning to risk seeking nurturance from her husband. (And it is a risk of great pain, considering his personality and her current need and sensitivity.)

The women referred to have been able to fulfill themselves and to enrich others to an unusual degree. As a result of the conditions prevailing in their original families, they have been able to avail themselves of the "two sources" for ". . . the possibilities of gratification . . . direct instinctual satisfaction and the . . . relationship to the environment, a relationship that grows gradually more independent of sexual instincts"[9] and that culminates in strong ego achievements. While direct sexual satisfaction may be tied to the female anatomy, the passive receptive attitude does not seem to be required of women in those relationships to the environment that have become independent of the sexual instinct. The mature individual, according to Binstock, feels "free of any *need* to sexualize anything . . . except lovemaking."[10] This appears to be especially true in an era when most activities, even those related to survival, are no longer directly dependent on either male or female physical attributes. Human intelligence has created tools and procedures that increasingly liberate men and women from the limitations of their nature. So far, conception and gestation remain exceptions, but the *pleasures* of sexual intercourse can be separated from the natural biological *consequences* of sexual congress. The beginning of cultural changes resulting from these technological advances are already evident. The deeper psychological consequences have not clearly emerged. But no woman now *needs* to use all her energies in the service of her sexual role. Although temperament and other constitutional factors may lead some women to choose generally passive aims, it seems evident that certain combinations of life experiences can become welded into a driving force determining an alternate life-style, which permits some others to confine their passive-receptive feminine aims to successful sexual relationships, while functioning in different spheres as active, assertive, even aggressive human beings.

Chapter 7

WOMEN AND CAREER GOALS: SOME DEVELOPMENTAL VICISSITUDES

Harriette Podhoretz, Ph.D.

"Leben and Arbeiten" (Loving and Working) are how Freud cryptically summarized the goals of psychoanalysis. Disorders in loving and working are painful and connected; yet up until recently psychoanalysis did not have a clear-cut mandate for the consideration of women's work inhibitions. Our culture may have served to disguise recognition of underlying issues of work conflicts among women in much the same way that the sympton of weight loss due to a low-cholesterol diet might mask a more insidious pathology, such as diabetes or cancer. The educated or accomplished woman who experienced a gap between her accomplishments and employment of these skills would not be considered as clinically suspicious as a man in such a position.

Although women have sought analytic therapy in the same proportion as men, the major goals of their treatment have not included uncovering aspirations or encouraging the achievement of financially or emotionally more rewarding careers. Nonetheless, many women did manage to experience the joy of being successful as an indirect result of therapy, because of the subtle yet powerful process of identification with a "good enough"[1] analyst. Until the middle of the 1960s, the relationship between the psychology of women and careers was not considered a worthy enough issue within traditional psychoanalytic thinking to warrant theoretical or clinical speculation. In this area, psychoanalysis seems to owe a major debt to psychology, by focusing on female achievement and women's ego functions and conflicts. The major thrust in the psychology of women has been the study of strivings to achieve in different populations of women, which has further defined the variables that contribute to achievement-orientation.

Psychologists operate very differently from psychoanalysts; they use objective tests and controlled experimentation to differentiate between and among groups regarding given variables (e.g., career aspirations of women). Psychoanalysts, on the other hand, work on the particular psychopathological arrests and conflicts that inhibit or restrict a woman from being able to engage in competitive work.

Psychologists formulate hypotheses, test in groups, and determine the significance of results through controlling different variables. Psychoanalysts, too, formulate hypotheses, test them through interpretations of the transferences,[2] resistances,[3] and defenses,[4] and then determine their significance, based on behavioral and personality changes. Thus, both disciplines approach the individual in vastly different ways. Few psychologists are familiar with analytic theory, and most psychoanalysts are unfamiliar with objective psychological studies. Therefore, my purpose here is to integrate the findings of objective psychology about women's career aspirations with the insights of psychoanalytic theory.

Mattina Horner's [5] seminal study of women's motivation for achievement discovered the phenomenon appropriately labeled the "motive to avoid success" and had the impact of a miniearthquake on the world of psychological research. It stimulated a host of other studies in which the attitudes and fantasies of women about achievement and competition were carefully investigated. In the last decade there have been numerous research projects about the conflicts that women experience in connection with their aspirations for careers.

A brief overview of some of the significant findings and theories should indicate the direction of recent research. Based on data from several of her projects, Horner[6] theorized that most men and women felt that " . . . competition, independence, competence, intellectual achievement, and leadership reflect positively on mental health and masculinity, but are basically inconsistent or in conflict with femininity." Significantly, some college women fantasized that if they were successful they would be attacked by their female peers, while others suffered mutilation or annihilation, and still others the loss of the love of significant male figures because of a reduction of their feminine appeal.

Somewhat earlier, McClelland[7] and Winterbottom[8] also used projective tests to link early childhood experiences of primary affective associations that involved the mother's attitude toward independence, mastery, and caretaking with the later character traits of achievement and competency. Veroff,[9] a student of McClelland, suggested that the development of motivation for achievement in females required a somewhat rejecting (i.e., not overly nurturant) attitude by the mother when the girl was young, and an appropriate timing of stress and mastery in middle childhood. Bardwick[10] agreed with Veroff and hypothesized a paradigm for the achieving female. In this model, the achieving girl has become significantly independent of her parents, with particular emphasis on independence from the mother, and has a nurturant and supportive father. A further study by Podhoretz,[11] using two objective and one projective instrument, found that achieving females had mothers who clearly and unambivalently allowed their daughters to compete with a standard of excellence, and fathers who were neutral regarding their daughter's success.

The major significance of these studies, both in terms of data and further theoretical speculation, is that they relate women's orientation toward achievement to the relationship of the self (including superego and ego ideal) with significant others, primarily in terms of the early emotional experiences within the nuclear family. Recently, sensitive and highly sophisticated psychoanalytic research has been conducted (utilizing both clinical and group data) about the young child's relationship to the mother, and later on to the father, and the impact of this early experience on subsequent ego functions and strivings for achievement.

Two major psychoanalytic theorists, Margaret Mahler[12] and Edith Jacobson,[13] have arrived at convergent theories regarding the psychological development of the child. They worked separately, Mahler through observation and construction, Jacobson clinically, with data reconstructed from patients' memories of their childhood.

Basically, they found that the developing child has internalized images or representations of herself/himself and others (mother, and later father). These images or representations are continually being modified, given normal development, to conform with the real picture of the self and each parent. Subsequently these images and their relationship to each other will, in complex ways, determine motives and efforts to achieve. These images are formed from within and become part of the structure of the unconscious. Yet these internal images, which figure in fantasies, often operate below the threshold of consciousness, and they are primarily responsible for inhibiting achievement or, conversely, advancing the proper development of ego functions and self-actualization.

Bridging the gap between psychological and psychoanalytic theory requires the sensitive correlation of large, group studies with data from the clinical case material of individuals who were viewed through a psychoanalytic framework. From there, theoretical formulations regarding the psychodynamics of behavior can be conceptualized and constructed.

Mahler and others, utilizing a group of normal infants and their mothers, conducted a field observation-type research project within the framework of the psychoanalytic concept of object-relations theory.[14] This study was longitudinal and helped to formulate her concept of the "psychological birth of the human infant."

Briefly, Mahler finds that the crux of her work centers on the concept of the separation and individuation of the child from the mother,[15] which includes an important subphase, rapprochement, in which the child ambivalently goes back and forth between separation-individuation and symbiosis.[16] Central to Mahler's thinking is that if the mother-child dyad is loving enough, the child will strive to achieve separation from her, a process the "good-enough" mother will not only tolerate, but also encourage. This separation or awareness by the child of its own "separateness" is the crucial precondition for important and complex ego functions that can and do foster optimal growth of self.

The disorders resulting from the failure of separation-individuation are often due to the child's inability to realize that the mother who nurtures and loves is also the one who shows disapproval. Therefore, the child's primary task is integration, and the child must learn that the mother who is loved is also the one who is hated (i.e., there is only one mother, as opposed to two). If the child cannot negotiate this crucial developmental task, a split in the image of the mother, the self, and reality will occur, in which the "good" mother is internalized and the "bad" mother is thrown off or "projected" onto the outside world. This fragmentation, or splitting, will then seriously interfere with all subsequent reality-testing and ego functions.

Another important theorist in the field of object relations is Edith Jacobson, who accepted the same matrix as Mahler (i.e., the mother-child dyad) and elaborated her own view of the development and discovery of identity in terms of infantile, preoedipal, and oedipal phases.[17] Initially the infant, as he or she proceeds through these developmental stages, experiences vacillating and contradictorily strong emotions directed toward both herself or himself and others, the mother initially, and later the father. The emotions of love and hate (libido and aggression) are intense and jarring; they must be tamed enough so that love outweighs hate. When the violent swings have sufficiently subsided (due to the fact that the self as well as the images have become consolidated with more love than hate), the child will be capable of developing lasting emotional attachments.

Here Jacobson also arrives at the developmental concept of "total" images of self and others that are forged out of the initial matrix of maternal love. These emotional investments manifest themselves through conscious, selective identifications, primarily with each parent, and then with others. When libidinal and aggressive feelings toward the self and others are integrated and the individual is faced with action, the loving feelings extend not only toward the various functions of the body, but also to the whole self. This increase of self-esteem puts the drive in motion and, "in the course of successful actions, intense rich feelings of identity are frequently experienced."[18]

Jacobson further theorized that if a split develops between intensely loving feelings toward the inner representations of mother or father, with a hateful attitude toward the self, the result ". . . is bound to produce failure and corresponds to masochistic or self-destructive behavior."[19] Any other disproportions of aggression over libido in terms of the self and others ". . . eventually leads to inactivity or to general inhibition of ego activity."[20] Jacobson summarizes by stating that ". . . all activity that an individual engages in must combine and utilize the energies derived from a relatively harmonious internalized relationship."[21]

A subsequent level, the oedipal stage, is a time when the child is at the height of rivalry with the parent of the same sex in competition for the other. A resolution of this phase brings successful

> . . . ego maturation, improved reality testing and self-awareness and expanding functional ego activities. Gradually toning down the child's imagery to a much more realistic level, they modify the child's wishful aggrandized self images and transform them into ambitious but realistic object-directed goals by blending them with corresponding parental ego goals. Depending on the parents' personality, they may extend to all kinds of parental interests and attitudes, their

ambitions and expectations for the child's future. Thus they may involve such aims as . . . intellectual, vocational . . . success and the like.[22]

Moreover, Jacobson stresses that in the child's development the preoedipal, oedipal, and adolescent experiences of the vicissitudes of love and hate play a very crucial role. It is also her impression that the functions involved in "work" utilize more of the loving or libidinal feelings than of aggressive ones, which tend to act as the prohibitions of conscience (i.e., superego). Nevertheless, she stresses that in activity or the ability to work productively, the most important factor is the relative proportion of these two drives.

Stating the above somewhat differently, work inhibitions and self-destructive behavior involving work goals and aspirations can be considered the expression (i.e., crystallizations and precipitates of unconscious conflicts that arose from both the preoedipal and oedipal phases of development). The traumatic crises that precipitated these arrests and conflicts may be buried in memory or, if remembered, appear to be disassociated from current work inhibitions. The particular traumas or losses, if stemming from the preoedipal stage, may center around various anxieties involving separation-individuation fear, such as abandonment by the mother, or may come from the later subphase of rapprochement—the sensitive, testing phase when the child wishes to be autonomous, but also wants to be able to return to the parent for approval of her or his other efforts. Sometimes these traumas involve the actual loss or death of a parent at either the preoedipal or oedipal stage. Other struggles can revolve around forbidden identifications, which are caused by a parent exploiting the loyalty of a child to prevent the child from identifying with the other parent. Also, feelings of competition and rivalry, arising from the later oedipal phase, give rise to fantasies and distortions about the self and others if they are not relatively well resolved. These distortions regarding the self and reality are the result of splitting the good and bad self, as well as good and bad "others" (i.e., mother and father). The failure to integrate love and hate deprives the ego of the energy required for self-fulfillment. Practically speaking, this means that the ego cannot develop and exercise self-enhancing skills and functions. The natural heirs to successful integration are joy and pleasure in accomplishment.

These developmental phases and their vicissitudes necessarily affect the achievement strivings and career choices of women. If, during the early stages of her development, a girl successfully masters separation-individuation and develops relatively firm internal boundaries between the self and others, she will have enough accrued energy to make important selective identifications with the admired and loved qualities of each parent. Also, enough energy is available for intellectual, cognitive, and aesthetic pursuits. If an unimpeded separation occurs in the preoedipal stages there will also be fewer disturbing fantasies (i.e., distortions regarding the self and others), and more realistic appraisals of the self and the world can be both formed and modified.

Therefore, when the girl approaches the oedipal conflict and the vicissitudes inherent in its negotiation, she does not have to sacrifice her efforts to achieve. At the height of her competitive relationship with the mother for her father's love, the girl need not fear vengeful retaliation or abandonment, which would force her to propitiate her mother by giving up her competence and strivings for success. Instead, she can selectively identify with the mother's admirable qualities, such as her femininity, and simultaneously retain her father's love, as long as he, too, does not reject her for being competent and successful. In fact, the process of selective identification is furthered because she is now encouraged to identify with his admired traits[23] also. Therefore, the two most powerful obstacles to successful struggles for success, loss and abandonment by the mother and rejection by the father, no longer function as impediments in the exercise of ego functions such as skills, intellectual expertise, and strivings. It is this type of pre-oedipally tinged oedipal conflict that is most relevant to women's work inhibitions.[24]

The psychoanalyst is faced not with a group, but with one distressed human being, a woman, reporting work inhibitions and career aspirations that appear to be frustrated. The treatment must delicately and sensitively explore and reconstruct the early and later childhood phases that gave rise to those specific developmental conflicts. Throughout the course of treatment, these conflicts reveal themselves through associations and memories, and they are pinpointed at their corresponding preoedipal and oedipal nodal points. Hopefully, they will eventually be worked through, and this resolution will result in a more integrated self, with a preponderance of love over aggression and more energy available for meaningful goals.

The following clinical case material will illustrate some of the above-mentioned theoretical points. The three women described below come from very different ethnic and sociocultural backgrounds. However, they share some strong similarities. All three have demonstrated academic competence and have expressed a desire for a professional or top-level career. Also, all have been inhibited, in varying degrees, due to fantasies regarding the self and others. These unconscious fears and wishes incorporated preoedipal fears of loss and abandonment, due to problems arising out of the process of separation-individuation, which were then condensed with the oedipal fears of destruction and retaliation.

D, a 32-year-old professional woman had a twofold goal; achieving a doctorate in the Social Sciences and becoming a university professor. Her mother brutally beat her daily from the age of 6 until 16. The beatings began when her father left home and ended when he terminated his job as a merchant seaman; then the family was physically united for the first time in 10 years and emigrated to the United States. While she was in her native country, D took highly competitive examinations and entered an intellectually elite school. For the next few years she failed one or two courses a semester, but received very high marks in her other subjects. At no time did she fail the same subject; excellence in one field simply meant failure in another. College in the United States was a repetition of high school. Graduate school was somewhat different; her straight A average was punctuated with marks of "Incomplete" due to a severe work inhibition in writing the required papers. As D. remembers and reconstructs her parents' attitudes toward her school work, she became aware of her mother's ambivalence. Her mother's physically abusive treatment alternated with special treats of food.[25] D's constructions were that her mother did not want her to succeed in school; otherwise she would not have mockingly said, as she beat her, "There sits my genius." Father, on the other hand, valued learning and was a Sunday scholar himself; he held out the promise of intellectual achievement for his daughter, even putting aside a fund "for your Ph.D." One of the precipitating causes for D's entering treatment was the moment of terror, a sense of fragmentation and annihilation, that she experienced when a graduate professor told her that she "belongs at Yale." His statement crystallized her preoedipal and oedipal fears and strivings, in which the terror of mutilation and reprisals were fantasied replays of the beatings she had actually experienced and wished to perpetrate upon her mother. In addition, success invoked the fear of loss and abandonment by her mother for being successful. Success in graduate school would culminate in getting not only a Ph.D., but her father too, albeit at a bloody price. The incompleted papers became the newly displaced, primitive arena in which the terrorizing skirmishes with her mother were to be relived and repeated. The papers now represented the unresolved, symbolic preoedipal and oedipal battles of the self with others. Autonomy and separation from her mother formerly meant her not surrendering to any demands from authority. Due to these early developmental traumas, she was left with an extremely unintegrated and unrealistic self-image: a bad, beaten, dirty, competitive self, as well as an idealized, aggrandized self. Disproportionate amounts of aggression and love directed at her self and the internalized representations of her mother and father resulted in insufficient energy for her to accomplish other tasks, such as the necessary completion of her papers. The course of her analytic treatment largely consisted of interpretations, through transference, of her distorted representations of herself as well as others. This woman was helped to integrate and modify her own self-image, incorporating more loving feelings toward herself, and exploring the source of the hateful and erotic feelings that had formerly interfered with her schoolwork. Most recently, a memory returned in which her father, on his bimonthly visits, was remembered as having worked on a school bench that he found and was fixing for her use. She recalled that it, like her papers, was never completed. With the return of this memory, she was able to begin reading for her papers. These and similar fantasies had prevented her from regarding work in a relatively neutral way (i.e., as a task) that she, a competent, intelligent woman, could master.

P is a 26-year-old black woman who works as a researcher for a newspaper. Her goal is reporting. She won a scholarship from a prestigious graduate school of journalism and showed great promise in her field assignments. She has also received excellent feedback from her colleagues and superiors at work.

Her problems were depression and inhibition in her social, sexual, and work life. She also experienced inhibition in completing and submitting resumés for jobs in her field.

P's mother grew up in the South, receiving little more than a third-grade education. After marriage to her father, a cab driver, who was a very light-skinned mulatto, the family settled in a black ghetto in New York. She persistently told P that she was her best friend and that if she didn't "stick by her mama" she would have no one. P's mother did not encourage her academic career and success but, instead, saw it as a prospective threat to their relationship, which would separate them.

When P was 16, her father died. She recalls him as a hard-working taxi driver who taught her how to play golf and considered her a buddy. Her job was to wake him up when he fell asleep on the toilet and lead him back to bed. He teased and devalued her mother by mocking her blackness and big breasts. Early in treatment, P recalled being told by her mother that when she was a child, she had a white friend, who eventually rejected her as "just a nigger." P was a mulatto like her father, and had ambivalent feelings about being less black than her mother.

In P's case the mother presented too little competition. She also let her daughter know that if she were successful, it meant separating from her. Success then meant intolerable isolation and abandonment. The fantasized fears and wishes that would result from success (i.e., superseding her mother and realizing incestuous cravings toward father), inhibited and confused this talented woman. An early unconscious identification with the mother around a "nigger" self, as well as a guilty incestuous self based on oedipal strivings, contributed to a bad self-image that made it difficult for P to achieve.

Treatment focused on P's self-image and its tendency to blur and fuse with her internalized image of her mother. For instance, she was a tall, slim, small-breasted, and beautifully groomed woman. However, any rejection or setback in her life would distort her image of herself. She would then experience herself as fat, big-breasted, and unattractively dressed, creating a depression due to a flux in her self-esteem, whereby her image of herself merged with mother's. Consistent work on these blurred, confused, and distorted images resulted in a more defined, more integrated, and more cohesive self. With the stabilization of her self-esteem, P felt more entitled to command recognition for her work as well as increased freedom to display her skills and competence. As the image of herself became more integrated, it also became more differentiated from the representation of mother, with fewer fantasies regarding abandonment for achievement.

R, a 28-year-old attractive, bright, and articulate woman, works in the news media. Her problems were depression and work inhibition, including an inability to write resumés for more important and better-paying jobs. She also experienced difficulties in studying for the law boards. Her immediate reason for initiating treatment was a severe depression coupled with a physiological regression, both due to a failure to receive a promotion. At this point she required catheterization because of an inability to urinate. R comes from a lower-middle-class, Italian-American background and has a brother 5 years her junior. Her mother is described as a compulsive, bitter, and disappointed woman; her father is an easy-going type who drinks heavily. She recalls her childhood as a time of vicious, frequent battles between her parents.

Even though her brother did poorly in school and never went to college, R distinctly felt that he was more valued than she, particularly by her mother. By contrast, R's grades were superior throughout school, including honors in college and an award for academic excellence. She remembers how mortified she felt when her father showed up drunk for this special occasion and how this incident provoked a battle between her parents, with her mother pointedly stating that father had no interest in his daughter's education. R felt that she has been put on the spot. If she defended her father against her mother, she abandoned herself; if she sided with her mother, she became identified with traits she despised and would have to turn on her father.

R acted out her fear of achievement by regressing back to an earlier stage that symbolically expressed a yearning for an early (preoedipal) mother and the prized penis (catheterization), which would make her more valuable in her mother's eyes. Moving backward also removed her from oedipal strife. Being faced with competition and loss in a present life situation revived unresolved infantile and competitive strivings with her brother as well as oedipal rivalries with mother. Success and competition were too frought with primitive aggressive and libidinal strivings that activated "bad" self and parental images.

In the course of her analysis R recaptured a memory of how when she was 18 her father kissed her passionately on the lips. This memory, when revived and explored in the context of her oedipal struggles, liberated her energies so that she was able to take her boards. Treatment here focused on the image of a "corroded self." This peculiar term, when explored, yielded the conscious awareness that her instinctual demands made her feel "wicked" and "whorish" (her mother's words). She had a split image of herself: a sweet, saintly girl-woman much like the parochial school student that she had been, and a whorish tart who wore makeup and liked sex. The work then focused on helping her to have an image of herself that was neither the unreal saint nor the unlikely sinner. When her jarring identifications fused into a more cohesive, modified, and loving self, energy previously bound up in warring images became available for realistic goals. Most recently she sought and won a prestigious and well-paid position.

In summary, psychological studies over the past decade have unearthed crucial data regarding women's desire for achievement and career goals. The findings indicate at least two important factors that bear on women's work inhibitions: early affective experiences within the mother-child dyad; and the nuclear family and women's fear of competition, based on fantasied fears of loss and rivalrous destruction.

Psychoanalytic research on autonomy and ego development has explored and substantiated these findings, but from within a framework that utilized the analysis and reconstruction of adult memories, as well as those of early familial relationships, stressing the strength of internalized representations on all subsequent ego activity. Mahler's research on child development found that the basis for optimum ego development rests on the construct of separation-individuation, while Jacobson, using the same developmental matrix, views ego development as a result of the preponderance of libido over aggression, the integration of which yields firm boundaries between the self and others.

Finally, the above-described clinical vignettes partially describe how analytic therapy, which stresses the buried conflicts at important preoedipal and oedipal stages, operates and may be considered appropriate treatment for woman's work inhibitions.

Chapter 8

THE MOTHER-ARTIST: WOMAN AS TRICKSTER

Jane Lazarre

THE RELIVING AND REUSING OF THE PAST

I am reading a recently published critical analysis of American women poets.[1] Early in the book, in the section on Emily Dickinson, who is now claimed as a foremother by so many writers and poets, the author observes:

> Most women choose to be "women": they remember, perhaps, the days of their youthful hopes for "Amplitude, or Awe"; they perhaps continue to dabble, perpetual amateurs. Of the few who have become artists and won the world's recognition, most have chosen as did Dickinson, sacrificing the traditional "feminine" role of wife and, *most certainly, of mother.* (my emphasis)

I read, for the second time, *To the Lighthouse* by Virginia Woolf, seeing themes I could not have noticed when I first read it at the age of 18. I am shocked at the way the major themes of my psychic life are articulated here by this poetic genius and feminist of the earlier half of the century: the internal development of the artist, Lily Briscoe, and the way she experiences her desire for love and her commitment to being a serious artist as utterly contradictory impulses; the yearning of the young girl, Cam Ramsey, for union with the adored father, the same father her brother sees as mercilessly autocratic, unrelentingly jealous and infantile; the perfect descriptions of the quintessential Mother, Mrs. Ramsey, her gaze and attention forever seeking the needs of others, of her children, her guests, her flowers, and especially of her husband. Only in the quiet evening does she rest, turn her vision inward, and experience a suggestion, never to be amplified or awesome, of the self.

Only when I am quite finished with the book do I allow myself to become conscious of its obvious truth: Lily Briscoe and Mrs. Ramsey are drawn in polar contrast to each other. It is Lily's decision, however touched by a sense of loss, to relinquish the possibilities of love and motherhood, that allows her to fulfill herself as an artist. Mrs. Ramsey has died mothering (". . . giving, giving, giving, she died."[2]). Lily Briscoe, "pulling her skirts tightly around her knees" in the face of a male (Mr. Ramsey's) demand for attention, callously turns back to her painting, refusing him her deepest attention. For Mr. Ramsey's demand for attention, Woolf makes painfully clear, is not different from a child's. The son—gazing at his father as an old man in the boat which, at the end of the book, is finally on the way to the lighthouse—was right. The father has always been the competitor of his children for the attention of the mother-wife, as most men continue to be today.

One night, after working very hard for weeks on a chapter for my current book, I am singing my son his traditional two lullabies before he goes to sleep. Suddenly he interrupts my song. "Mommy," he asks directly, "who do you love better, me or your writing?"

Question: Who am I to imagine that I can bring Lily Briscoe and Mrs. Ramsey together?

The mother who is an artist can never transcend the double self. The same double self is common to all mothers (in some sense, we all remain daughters), but it is intensified in the artist, because she is someone who has always been plagued by a double consciousness.

As a child, I had two voices—two girls spoke from within me. The first was the Me-Voice: honest, desperate, and loyal. The other one was the World-Voice: a saucy, troublesome, talkative girl who was either obeying the rules of convention with such orthodox rigidity that one could become sick just listening to her lies, or else spurting out some outlandish piece of nonsense she thought was "deep." The World-Voice, although it turned out to be mine as much as any other, seemed to belong to other girls, strange women, even an occasional man. Sometimes I would find myself running after that rash and disobedient creature who frequently stole the whole body for herself, running after her through the night, yelling: *Return the body to me immediately, I am here too!* She remained magnificently unconcerned. She knew the Me-Voice would not risk sound, and that gave her the edge.

Eventually the Me-Voice learned to write, if not always to speak. Borrowing the knowledge of grammar, the variety of vocabulary, and the respect for structure that the World-Voice accumulated so carefully over the years, the Me-Voice speaks (writes) for anyone who cares to hear.

But the Me-Voice is often uncontrolled, unrespectable, given to obsessional scepticism regarding truths most know to be proven or incontestable, truths such as: When children are in the oedipal stage of life it is overly provocative for their mothers to bathe with them and let them suck her breasts pretending they are babies again. But (whispers the Me-Voice) what if this sort of prolonged maternal sensuality, this delayed merging, can help ease the pain of separation, loosen the knotty cramps that notoriously accompany growth? The Me-Voice is not the "good-mother" voice as she is ordinarily defined. Children, according to such definitions, need clear limits, simple directions, consistent rules. I can believe this, but I often find it difficult to incorporate into my own life, especially if I have been working with energy and regularity (particularly regularity) on my writing. Habits carefully nurtured between 9 and 3:30, habits of keeping every possible inner light focused on contradiction, of allowing opposing forces to ramble inside at will, such habits are not easily folded like freshly washed towels and put away in the afternoon to wait neatly on the shelves until the following morning.

Writing, said Tillie Olsen in an essay called "Silences," involves the constant "reliving and reusing of the past."[3] But the past called forth daily over long periods of time does not nestle in for an afternoon nap—sleeping as deeply as a child—when it is time to become a mother again. In-stead, it is often very difficult to meet my young children on the ground of the present, unhampered in word, deed or gesture by the flailings of disturbing and sometimes evil ghosts.

The most visible and consistent occupant of my past is my mother. Long dead, she changes shape—even moves into altered meaning—through the cycles of my life, but she is always there. Women writers and poets have occasionally talked about the muse as a woman—as friend or as lover, but always beneath it all, as mother. The poet, Honor Moore, in a short piece on motherhood, spoke of her own mother and the women poets who are her spiritual mothers, poets such as Adrienne Rich, as her muses: those who give her permission to write.[4] For May Sarton, in *Mrs. Stevens Hears the Mermaid Singing,* it is always love for another woman that inspires poetry.[5] Long before I was conscious of it as an acceptable statement to be publicly admitted with the sounds of the World-Voice, I knew that my mother had always been my muse. When she was too real to me, becoming simply *the mother who died and abandoned me when I was small,* she prevented me from writing. During those times, I hide all her photographs, haunted as I am by her image too regularly and clearly in my dreams. Patiently (for I've been through three cycles now), I try to bury her again. When she is gone as my particular childish memory, she arises as my protector, the *Woman Who Gives Me Permission.* My closest women friends also partake of this function in my life—giving permission through empathy or identification to the Me-Voice to speak. They become my mother. And then I place my mother's picture back on the wall.

But my mother represents the dark side of life, from her own dark complexion which, after her death, was transformed by her grieving family into a sign of divinity, to the grave whose utter black absence of light tormented my childish nights. She became for me a witch and a queen,

Goddess of Night. The dark side can be expressed in various ways. I might actually be writing about death, despair, or anger, and then I often write smoothly—their expression comes most naturally to me. If I am writing about lighter subjects, more abstract ideas, or if I am writing humorously, then I can only write well if I am in touch with the underside of every thought, the unsayable, the slightly grotesque.

I think this is true for many women writers. Perhaps our lives as women, caretakers of the unpredictable, the uncontrollable, the emotional, have always been involved with the dark side. Artists as tricksters,[6] holders of emotional oppositions, and especially women artists, therefore, may live most intensely in that special dark, the unconscious often gaping and accessible. It may be for this reason, as well as any other, that women often write of the inner world. One tries, by expression, to sort out the deafening messages.

The temperament and personality of the underself, the one who is at once the most passionate and authentic self but also the disturbing, nagging onlooker, may vary. But whoever she is can neither be transcended nor overcome. She must be utterly accepted, loved, cherished. Although one struggles over the years to discipline her, one must finally let her be. For without her energy there will be no art. It is the nourishing of this underself that often makes motherhood difficult for the artist.

That demanding underself torments me at times, driving me into what can only be called bouts with madness. I may have the feeling of being overwhelmed by what I know to be fantasy, the fear that I am completely unrealistic and exaggerated in my perceptions. And yet I have no immediate power to discover a path to the real once again, although it may sit closely and visibly right beside me. But these bouts, it must be admitted, can become amazingly finite in mothers—a way in which the mother-person can strengthen the artist-person. I have heard women describe days of hysteria and loss of self that end promptly when it is time to pick up the children.

Adrienne Rich *(Of Woman Born)* has said that in patriarchal society all women (and men) come to feel "wildly unmothered,"[7] unprotected by the presence of a powerful, assertive mother. Wildly unmothered, I wish to wildly mother my children. I would be a wild cheetah clearing paths in the forest. Rarely calm. Never obedient. Ripping flesh for meat for myself and my young. The cheetah mother, loving passionately and intensely, born of the underself, comes easily to the artist-mother.

But I would also like to be a swan floating downstream, my wings spread gently enclosing ducklings, my head tilted upward, my black mouth serene. It is difficult for the artist-mother to call into regular being the swan-woman: she who is responsible, casual, certain, and in control. Sylvia Plath described the two faces this way:

> There are two of me now,
> this absolutely new white person and the old yellow one.[8]

One day, without warning, the old yellow one will pick the children up at school and live with them all through the evening. She walks through the door of the day-care center where her child has been for 7 hours. When the child screams in anger at the sight of her she knows this is because of the pain of transitions in his or her young life, from home to day care, from day care to home. She knows she must tolerate the hurtful onslaught. But instead of toleration, she finds infantile rage (she has been dipping her pen in that rage all day long; she has had a good day writing, which means the underself is still in control). She yells at her small child, mercilessly and publicly. Instead of becoming the swan-mother who protects and accepts, she too becomes a child. More siblings than mother and child, they rage at each other until both hearts are quieted. Only later will she hold the child and love him with equal intensity. The extremes of her behavior result partly from the fact that as an artist she can never fully bury her past or repress emotional oppositions.

Knowing all this, I continue to wish that I could be for my children the absolutely new white person; when I am, I feel a sense of exoneration, the sense of self-congratulatory accomplishment and humorous pride of the Trickster, turned suddenly from Earthmaker, Creator of the Universe, into some being of the forest, fooling everyone with His ordinariness.

The other day, my 3-year-old son was angry because my lap, which he feels to be his private possession, his permanent prize for being the baby of the family, was occupied by his brother. The older one rarely sits on my lap any more and I was warm and glad to have him there, although his long legs hang down to the ground and his 75 pounds threaten to take the breath from me. The 3-year-old rages on, and finally I send him to his room to rage away from his brother's and my embrace. This week I feel it is the older one who needs more attention, who has been neglected too often. Soon the 3-year-old returns, still crying, to the side of my chair, clutching his blanket and peering into his brother's victorious eyes. I hold the young one's hand while allowing the older one to remain in my lap. I tell my baby, "I still love you when I'm holding Adam. Don't you think I love Adam when I'm holding you?" He nods yes. Then I say quietly (oh, quietly, and with a nicely proportioned maternal authority), "Adam may be real big to you, but he's still a little boy too. He needs his mommy to hold him too. Don't you want Adam to be held sometimes?" The little one bursts into cries again, face to face with his ambivalence.

Then my older son gets off my lap on his own and puts his brother in his place. While the little one cuddles in, the older boy—that firstborn, that self of myself (there is a whole literature to be written by mothers on the differences between the firstborn and the others), the older boy embraces his brother, the very baby he once claimed to hate, the baby who for dreams on end was run over by cars, thrown out of windows, left to bleed in abandoned houses. Now he is truly embraced. And his big brother, searching for a sign of his own disadvantage, says with conviction, "You don't have to be jealous. I may be older but your birthday comes first in the year!"

For the 15 minutes my rather small body can stand their combined weight, we all nestle into the chair, me, open and motherly, on the bottom. But for 3 days I walk with medals weighing me down. There is a monument erected in my honor on the corner of the block. I am crowned Queen of the Universe.

The next morning I will try once again to go deep into pits of darkness holding my mother's hand, and I am afraid that tomorrow at 3:30 the untranslated oppositions, the memories of infancy, the burning illicit desires, will not be folded and put away as easily.

DAILY LIFE

Joseph Conrad said that in order for writing to go well, "the flow of daily life (must be) made easy and noiseless."[9]

This remark of Conrad's is quoted by Tillie Olsen in her essay on silences in writer's lives, she who herself had a long, tormenting silence. "In the twenty years I bore and raised my children," she says, "[I] usually had to work on a job as well, the simplest circumstances for creation did not exist."[10]

When she did write, she dared to write about the life she knew, the daily life of mothering. In *I Stand Here Ironing*, she writes of an eldest child:

> I stop the ironing. What in me demands that goodness in
> her? And what was the cost, the cost to her of such good-
> ness?
>   . . . Let her be. So all that is in her will not bloom—but
> in how many does it? There is still enough to live by. Only
> help her to believe that she is more than this dress on the
> ironing board, helpless before the iron.[11]

I can never read this passage without tears. But even
now writing about "female" experience, such as mothering, is considered a less serious topic for literary attention
than, for example, the "human" experience of war.

Today there is a feminist movement, other women, to
give support. But still, the idea of an easy and noiseless
daily life is a ludicrous anachronism to a mother of young
children, artist or not. The direct opposite is the case.
Sometimes I feel as if I am climbing over mountains of
soiled clothing, plowing my way through jungles of enormous Tinker-Toy trees, little Lilliputian superheroes all
around me, pulling my ankles, trying to make me stumble
or fall. Up ahead, across the sea, mammoth lists await me.
They reach into the sky, their demanding authority far
more terrifying than Moses's tablets. Buy green vegetable
for dinner. Take Adam to art lesson. Get sitter for Friday
night. Type announcements for day-care fund raiser and
xerox for 35 parents. As I stare, my arms begin to itch with
the familiar anxiety rash that accompanies the "viewing of
lists."

But the list is on the other side of the sea. I must not
think of it until 3:00. Until then I must forget the jungles
and mountains threatening always to pull me into their
depths. (The meat needs defrosting. The boys' room is a
mess. Where have I put Adam's jacket? It has turned cold
since this morning.) Forget them. Look only ahead at the
sea through which I may gracefully swim until 3:00, on
whose waves and nourished by whose depths I may find one
beautiful sentence.

My beautiful sentences are lost the moment I allow myself to focus on the desires of children that I do not fulfill. Trying to find a new sort of smooth transition between an intellectual insight and a hidden emotion, I think the following instead.

They want me to bake cookies with them. Mathew's mother bakes cookies with him. But then I must *plan* to bake. Another list. I must: buy the ingredients (sublist: flour, eggs, sugar, chocolate. And I never know whether or not I need baking soda or vanilla once I am in the store so in my cupboard, testimony to the infrequency with which I bake, stand eight little jars of vanilla, ten cans of baking soda). This list of ingredients involves two different stores (sub-sublist: Food City for basics, the little Spanish grocery store on the corner for the specially flavored candles they like). After planning to bake, I must find a wide afternoon to engage in the complicated activity of baking with children. I will have to keep a watchful eye on them so that each gets a turn, not letting the little, anxious fingers overturn the bowls of milk and light yellow eggs; there will be much cleaning after it is all done.

It would be lovely to bake cookies with them every week, I think stubbornly as I try to find the lost channel to the writing source. I wish I could do it in order. Close my journal. Neatly stack my papers on a corner of my desk that has been wiped clean of blood stains, dusted of particles of falling skin, and say, "Ah, Saturday morning. Time to bake cookies."

I rarely bake cookies. Will they suffer and hate me? Who, if not I, will lead their small hands, wonderful in themselves to lick, over to dough for kneading? If they hate me when Johnny's mother bakes cookies, I will say, "Remember that time we went to Kentucky Fried Chicken on Broadway and brought home the Extra Crunchy you liked so much?"

Shall mothering be measured by four bowls of remem-

bered ingredients stacked superciliously against some un-
nutritious pieces of Kentucky Extra Crunchy Fried
Chicken?

Daily life is often a problem. One day I completely
forgot to take my older son to his art lesson. Unable to find
the phone number of his artist-teacher, I called her mother
(also a friend) whose number I did have. I apologized for
my forgetfulness and asked for her daughter's number.
And the mother, an actress and writer, said to me, "Don't
worry. My children are 30 and 27 years old and I still wake
in the night from nightmares about forgetting to bring one
to a dance class, forgetting to pick up the other."

Pajamas go unmended. I meant to teach them to clear
their own plates from the table, but I find I do it myself.
Like all mothers, I find the enormous quantities of details
related to child rearing always getting the best of me, elud-
ing my plans for organization. But if I am to work at my art,
I must struggle to keep my mind as free as possible—to
seek connections where I had not seen connections before,
to find the proper tone in which to speak, because if I don't
find the tone, I will lose the content. I fight to keep my mind
free, and then I yell instead of leading gently when one of
my sons makes silly mistakes on his math homework, mistakes that come from a tendency to think about baseball
when he *ought* (the very ought that tormented my childhood) to be concentrating on math.

"Sloppy attitude," I said crisply the other day over his
chicken-scratch handwriting.

"Sloppy attitude," they said to me while I silently
swore that I would never say such things to children. This
cannot be what Tillie Olsen meant when she spoke of the
"reliving and reusing of the past."

One other aspect of "daily life" can catch the mother-
artist in a maze that turns her round and round, offering no
exit, becoming more and more frustrating in its insolubility
as she wanders into its dead-end doors. It is the Money
Maze.

I am an artist who makes very little money, and when I do make a barely adequate amount, it is always irregular and unpredictable. Whether or not there is a man present, most women with families work, either by choice or by need, usually a combination of both. Few can make a predictable living from art, and children's needs are relentlessly predictable: each season they grow out of their clothes; each summer they want to go to camp; each Christmas they want the same toys as their friends. I consider the possibility of getting a "real" job. But then I will have no time to write, only to work the job and mother. I will have to suffer long silences that will bring in their wake an inner turmoil that becomes at best fury, at worst the madness that comes when artists do not create art. People, after all, become artists not only from conscious rational choice, but from deep emotional need. I must write. I must mother. Then I cannot get a job.

If the mother has a young child, she goes into the wing of the maze labeled: Absence of Free Child Care. She cannot work on her art, even intermittently, unless she has child care. She cannot get child care without money. She cannot get money by working on her art. She is caught.

If the mother has older children, she is better off. She gets free child care 5 hours a day. On weekends the child can be persuaded to leave her alone for several hours. But she must still wander in the maze entitled: Inadequate Income and Insufficient Time. Sometimes it takes me hours to prepare to write. I may read, write long passages in my journal, try to focus my thought on the subject I am writing about, find the inner channel. Sometimes the gears do not shift so efficiently. After 4 hours, I am ready to begin. But then, in a half hour it will be time to pick up the children.

Daily life, endlessly complicated and horribly noisy, stalks my patience, obliterating any sign of maternal excellence, or drowning me in the very sea from which I had futilely hoped to fish out my one beautiful sentence.

THE GIFTS

But there are gifts the children receive from their mother-artist-woman, and I am being trained by my living mother-sisters to spot the gifts as well as the hardships that I give children.

First Gift: *The Turning of a Car Into a Painting*

I dream I am in a car driven by my husband. He cannot find a parking spot and is becoming more and more frustrated. We are in front of my old home, the apartment in which I grew up and down. He searches and searches, and finally finds a spot, but then the car is too large for the small city spot. Although I cannot drive—am frightened by the mechanical power under my hands—I say, "Don't worry. I'll drive the car for you." I take the wheel and, under my hands, the car becomes a painting, the one I loved to draw and look at as a child. Now I am holding the painting, trying to find the right spot for it on a clear, white wall. This turning of a car into a painting is a gift for my children. I am trying not to fear my own power, and it is the steady working on my art that gives me that pride. I will wildly mother and not turn them so quickly over to the authorities who warn of too much mother-love, and I will say to them, with the poet, Robin Morgan: "You shall be a child of the mother and your face shall not be turned from me. . . ."[12]

Second Gift: *The Father as Grownup*

I mean to distinguish between the maternal function with respect to children, who require some kind of daily, consistent mothering, and to men who ought not to require it in such large doses. If I am to be an artist and a mother and also live with a man, I cannot also manage being a mother to my husband in the traditional sense. He must care for his own clothes, plan family meals and activities as often as I do, remember his own phone numbers and dates, and spend several nights a week alone or at least without me while I meet with writers or others who feed my work. I, of course, must offer him the same space in return, but then women have always been expected to do so. He must learn, as I had to, to respond to the emotional needs of children and to sacrifice the needs of work to the needs of children when this is necessary. He must learn to glory in my successes and take my failures, of nerve and of performance, utterly seriously. The husband as grownup. A father for a boy to admire. A father who does not remain, in the words of Adrienne Rich, "essentially a son."[13]

Third Gift: *My Need for Them*

I am deeply frightened of the time when my children will leave me. The dark cheetah, the very one who juggles inner oppositions and rearranges them into art, mocks any convenient and facile assertions like, "Children must all leave and I will cope with it. I am, after all, not neurotically attached. . . ." The dark cheetah, turning her back, listens instead to the warnings of older mothers.

"When they leave," said a friend, "the adjustment is worse if you can imagine it than when they first come."

"What will be left," I ask my sons silently, "when you have taken yourself into the world, the little men you have become acting as sturdy captains of what was once my own small vessel? *The important thing is independence. I raise you to leave me.* I will be thrown overboard, back into the icy sea I swam in before you came. What do you leave me, cruel one? I will be alone again. The past returned. *Never you mind. Live your life.* Each new separation causes anguish in me, preventing my life, that once well-defined entity, from going on as before. In any separation we can lose each other. In any separation. Climbing rocks. Going to camp.

Crossing streets. Growing up. Willing your life heedless of my warnings. There is no separateness here. And yet I constantly struggle to be separate, to let them be. This is my final gift. My unalterable need for them.

The mother who is an artist can never transcend the double self. Some kind of compatibility has been achieved through the daily process of work. But motherhood demands a new sort of synthesis. Once again, the two selves must work together, but for different ends than they do in the service of art. The synthesis, then, is never permanent, but must be unbraided each morning and then, each afternoon, rebraided in a new pattern. The mother-artist is always trickster, becoming child, becoming animal, becoming god.

Chapter 9

SOCIOHISTORICAL AND PSYCHOANALYTIC PERSPECTIVES ON CAREER AND MOTHERHOOD

Alan Roland, Ph.D. and Barbara Harris, Ph.D.

A highly anomalous situation developed for many American middle-class and upper-middle-class women in recent decades as America became increasingly urban and industrialized—a situation that has received searching analyses. On one hand, these women were strongly encouraged throughout childhood, adolescence, and the college years to become well-educated and to achieve. On the other hand, upon reaching adulthood and marrying, they were completely relegated to the role of housewife-mother, with their desires for self-assertion and self-fulfillment, for achievement and development to be fulfilled vicariously through husband and son. They were expected to derive their sense of self from what they could do for others in the family instead of by focusing on their own self-development. The few women who decided to devote themselves to a career generally did so with a realization that their choice precluded marriage and children. This anomaly, reflecting profound cultural ambivalences, became more pronounced with World War II when, for the first time, many married women with children went into the work force and then continued to work after the war because of the pressures of inflation and rising economic expectations. The housewife-mother ideal and role still remained the cultural norm, with work mainly viewed as a means of helping out with family expenses. However many women found a new sense of achievement and recognition in their jobs.

From a psychological standpoint, these women were expected to work out an identity synthesis in adulthood almost exclusively around nurturing roles of mother and wife, of being there for others—the feminine mystique,[1] leaving out important identity elements from their whole previous schooling and development. For a number of women, this culturally sanctioned identity worked to various degrees. But for many, many others, leaving out important, developed parts of themselves created considerable anguish, unhappiness, and unrest. In a society characterized by the nuclear family except in certain ethnic groups, and with the exodus to the suburbs in the 1950s, the lot of the housewife-mother was often a lonely one as well.

From a historical perspective, this traditional identity of women is not a product of the sociocultural forces of the past few decades. The feminine mystique has important antecedents far preceding the post-World War II era. Nor is this identity God-given and eternal throughout human history either. Instead, the triumph of the middle class in the industrial revolution brought about profound changes in the family. Work and productivity shifted to the factory and business outside the home, basically for the first time. Men went away from the home to work in a highly competitive world, while middle-class women were to be protected at home, to take care of household and children—thus giving rise to the cult of domesticity. Deprived of participation in work and the status enjoyed from such productivity, as in preindustrial Western society, these women gained new status through the new emphasis on child care and their role as guardians of culture and ethics. In the home women were expected to create a calm haven from the swirling storms of the industrial revolution outside. The cult of domesticity also distinguished these women and their families from the lower classes, where women formed an important part of the new industrial labor force.

The social and cultural pressures in the United States to keep the cult of domesticity intact after World War II, in spite of the fact that an increasing number of middle-class women went to college and then to work, has been delineated with great clarity by Betty Friedan[2] and other feminist writers.[3] In the 1960s, the second women's movement was launched when a receptive audience composed primarily of middle-class women responded positively to these analyses in a social climate actively concerned with human rights and social reform. Historically feminist movements in the United States have coincided with and been given impetus by larger movements of social reform —such as the Abolitionist and Progressive movements. As a result of the women's movement in the 1960s, and even more so in the 1970s, an increasing number of women have sought out careers, and many are trying to combine them with motherhood as well—a dual-role identity rarely existing in prior decades.

As these women struggle to achieve an identity encompassing career and motherhood—until only recently considered to be mutually exclusive—a variety of social and psychological factors affect such a new integration, at times enabling considerable personal fulfillment to occur, at other times bringing about conflict, guilt, and anxiety. From a sociocultural standpoint, commitment to a career has traditionally been regarded as being opposed to the values and roles of the housewife-mother. Careers usually demand more involvement than most jobs, and, there is also an inner commitment to work as a means toward self-actualization. This obviously is in conflict with a mystique that a woman may only assert herself for others.

Crucial to any identity synthesis are the particular prevailing ideologies or value systems of a given historical era. To the extent that the prevailing ideology was against women working in careers, or even more against their having both a career and children, it was only the unusual woman who could manage both. At the present time, the woman's movement has created significant change in the ideological climate around work. While there are obviously still strong cultural norms and role expectations within American society for continuation of the cult of domesticity, there is far more room for evolving and living out different life-styles.

One important ideological factor that has been discussed at length by the feminists has been the traditional psychoanalytic viewpoint on women and femininity. Classical Freudian psychoanalysis emphasized psychosexual development, and any efforts for women to achieve in the work world were interpreted as a manifestation of penis envy or of a masculinity complex. To the extent that the concept was used to denigrate women's efforts at achievement in the arena of work, penis envy naturally became a *bête noire* to the feminist viewpoint.

The psychoanalytic orientation of this book takes off from other positions that have developed within the psychoanalytic and psychological fields, mainly over the last 25 years or so. It stresses the inherent human drive toward self-actualization, mastery, and new ego integrations, as developed by diverse writers such as Rank, the Menakers, Erikson, Maslow, Angyal, Fromm, White, and Rogers.[4] Thus, women's striving to realize themselves in work and career is viewed as a legitimate human need for self-actualization, and not as simply envying and imitating men. Maslow, whose major research was on self-actualization, went a step further. He actually warned many of the young women in his senior-year psychology courses in the 1950s that if they did not continue to develop their minds and themselves after graduating, neurosis and unhappiness would be their lot.[5] Self-actualization accords with a general human need to realize diverse potentialities—in women, often achievement in a variety of areas, while in men often to become more in touch with feelings and their capacity for nurturance. We view the striving for self-actualization as a more fundamental human motivation than the pleasure principle or the sublimation of drives—although the latter may be incorporated into the former. We further view self-actualization as fundamentally an ego need instead of an id one. We also consider self-actualization as more basic than Freud's principle of homeostasis—the reduction of tension through fulfillment of the drives—or even than Hartmann's concept of adaptation.[6] Self-actualization further accords with certain more positive aspects of the ideology of individualism—important in Western cul-

ture since the Renaissance, but heretofore usually restricted to men.

Our psychoanalytic viewpoint on the psychology of
women also encompasses contributions on identity conflicts and syntheses—particularly Erikson's and the Menakers' efforts to synthesize psychoanalytic data with those of
the social sciences on late adolescence and adulthood; and
a variety of contributions on the early development of the
self and narcissism—stemming from the early mothering
relationship with the child. Emphasis on this early relationship comes mainly from the contribution of a variety of
Freudian analysts working after Freud. We hypothesized in
the second chapter that the shift in psychoanalysis to inves-
tigations of the self and identity stems partly from profound sociocultural changes that have created significant
problems in the self or identity which make it far more
difficult for an individual to function in modern society.
Relevant factors around self and identity will be discussed
below as they affect career and motherhood.

Since psychoanalysis still exerts a powerful ideological
force within our society, three other issues must be discussed. One involves the concept of the superego or unconscious conscience, which Freud posited as being
inferior in women because it did not seem sufficiently rigorous, impersonal, and independent of emotional origins.
Contemporary psychoanalysts such as Applegarth[7] and
Bernstein (Chapter 5) have rethought this issue and con-
cluded that Freud mistook structure for content. Bernstein
further concludes that the woman's superego is extremely
strong, at times unbending, but it traditionally consists of
values and attitudes that compel the woman *not* to assert
herself in any way independently of others. Since the superego and ego-ideal develop in childhood and are major
unconscious transmitters of cultural values, they tend to
preserve the status quo. And when this occurs in a traditional family where the cult of domesticity and the feminine

mystique are predominant, this type of superego can become a major hindrance to women's being able to assert and realize themselves through a career. As Bernstein points out, such women may experience considerable anxiety over self-assertion and strivings to achieve, which interferes with their functioning in the work world. A traditional superego and ego-ideal can also generate enormous guilt when a woman tries to combine a career with motherhood. Only when there are supportive relationships in childhood for a woman to realize her own potentialities and assertiveness will a superego and ego-ideal develop more consonant with contemporary sociocultural opportunities.

A more recent ideological issue has developed from studies over the last two decades in psychoanalysis that have stressed the importance of the early mothering relationship and its effect on more severe psychopathology. The importance of empathy, emotional relatedness, and the nonintrusive support for the child's strivings for separation and individuation in early childhood have all been emphasized and developed by analysts such as Winnicott, Spitz, Kohut, and Mahler, to name just a few doing work in this area.[8] This has indirectly often led to an overemphasis on the mother as sole contributor to any problems the child may have, thus leaving the father out of the picture. Unfortunately, he often *has* been away in the traditional middle-class family, thus contributing significantly to whatever problems are present. In a more extreme way, certain analysts posit that it is crucial for the biological mother to take full care of the child on the assumption that this is necessary for a stable image and identification to take place without the undue arousal of anxiety. They further urge that careers should only be resumed after the child can at least go to nursery school. There is no question that such psychoanalytic positions arouse considerable guilt in many women seeking a dual-role identity, to the point that they question whether they should spend any time away from the infant and toddler. This, of course, is not our position, nor that of many other psychoanalysts.

From a more positive standpoint, psychoanalytic study has called attention to the great significance of the mothering of the infant and young child in the early development of the self. Our viewpoint is that adequate planning must be done to have such mothering carried out, but that it does not necessarily have to be all done by the biological mother, or even by women. Historically, child rearing in extended families has been done by a variety of women; today, more fathers than ever are involved in child care. A sense of inner emptiness develops in the child and later in the adult when there is really no one around to relate to the young child in an involved way; and other psychopathology occurs when there are pathological relationships present, such as strong intrusiveness. Either of these outcomes can be avoided without having the biological mother assume the whole burden of child care. A variety of workable arrangements can and have been worked out by the mother and father with each other and with others.

The third ideological issue is a controversial one. Drawing from the fields of biology and ethology, writers such as Alice Rossi[9] and Esther and William Menaker[10] (sociologist and psychoanalysts, respectively) postulate that while women should be given every opportunity and support for career fulfillment, and men should participate far more in child rearing, nevertheless women, on balance, are naturally probably more suited than men for the crucial mothering relationship with the infant. Many feminists do not go along with this biosocial approach, taking a position that roles are completely socially and historically determined and that men would be fully equal to women in the nurturance of the infant if the culture prepared them for that role. These feminists further argue that any position that states that women are on the whole more suitable for the nurturance of infants and young children evokes intense guilt over self-assertive strivings to work, and helps to cement the woman in the housewife-mother role. It also deprives men of an equal opportunity to enjoy and develop their role as fathers.

One thing does seem to be clear: any emphasis on women on the whole being intrinsically more suited for the nurturance of the infant stirs up considerable conflict today and becomes an important ideological issue in many women's identity synthesis. Anything smacking of older views arouses considerable anxiety and is experienced as pushing women into the Procrustean Bed of the cult of domesticity.

On the other hand, there are feminists who are strongly in favor of careers for women and women's right to achieve in the work world, but who believe that the women's movement has unwittingly identified with predominant male values in denigrating the importance of child-rearing, whether by women or men. In effect, they say only work and career are given value. These feminists believe a new balance is necessary, where child-rearing and career are each accorded full worth.

In the achievement of an identity synthesis, the presence of historical traditions, current cultural norms, and social role expectations and patterns are one crucial set of variables that individuals must cope with and integrate into their identity. Equally important is what has been internalized and developed in the psyche throughout childhood and adolescence. These more internal and often unconscious aspects are powerful although by no means completely determining elements in later identity integrations. They do, however, play significant roles in either generating support or creating conflict and guilt for women who strive to combine career and motherhood. From the chapters in this book, as well as from other literature on the subject, several factors seem identifiable.

One is the superego or unconscious conscience (the do's and don'ts internalized from the parental environment), and the ego-ideal (how I should and want to be, based on early idealizations that are internalized). To reiterate what was discussed above, to the extent that the superego and ego-ideal of the developing girl come from a traditional family structured around the cult of domesticity, then any self-assertive, self-actualizing, and independent strivings not related to filling others' needs would often be experienced as anxiety-arousing and would undermine her efforts in the work world. On the other hand, involvement with a career could also arouse intense guilt over not living up to the early ego-ideal of the perfect housewife-mother.

Another factor is the woman's early identifications with her own mother and the mother's attitudes toward her daughter, conscious and unconscious. As Menaker has stated in Chapter 4, many women from traditional families who are involved in careers have counteridentified with their own mothers; that is, they have rejected the model of the traditional housewife-mother for a more self-fulfilling and independent life involving work. However, early unconscious identifications have inevitably been made with these mothers. To the extent that they experience the mother in a denigrated or inferior role in the family, there is often a constant striving in their work life to offset any inner images of inferiority through unconscious identifications. On the other hand, upon having children, the unconscious identification usually becomes even more activated, and guilt and anxiety over having a career and not spending all one's time with the children may surface. Some of these problems should be significantly alleviated as new daughters have mothers who have worked out a dual-role identity.

There is still another facet of the mother-daughter relationship that constitutes an important identity element. In Chapter 5, Doris Bernstein posits that the mother-daughter relationship in early childhood is an extremely intense one because of the mother's narcissistic identification with the daughter as similar to herself, and the daughter's need to be close to the mother in order to make important identifications with her. But since the daughter also needs to separate and individuate from the mother, profound ambivalency conflicts often normally occur. In a traditional family, the daughter may also want to identify with the male who is given more freedom and independence as a way of separating from the mother. As Podhoretz describes in Chapter 7 in one case illustration, if a mother has unduly turned to her children for emotional sustenance and clings to them—a not infrequent occurrence in a traditionally structured family—then any striving of the daughter for independence and achievement may be fraught with the anxiety of abandonment by the mother, and intolerable isolation ensues. Anxiety over achievement may also be provoked if the mother experiences jealousy over her daughter's accomplishments and feels her daughter will therefore be favored by her husband.

Today, when the option for career and motherhood is much more available, there appears to be a number of women who are involved with careers and who either marry or are involved in long-term love relationships with men, but who do not want children. Involvement with motherhood is often consciously experienced as threatening their career fulfillment and, indeed, motherhood realistically could prevent them from moving ahead optimally in their vocation. Also present may be unconscious identifications with a traditional housewife-mother that may be deeply experienced as a profound threat to any career involvement. It is sometimes only when this unconscious identification is resolved that career and motherhood are experienced as being possibly congruent.

We have so far delineated important aspects of the mother-daughter dyad relevant to dual-role identity. The father-daughter relationship is no less crucial. From Charlotte Kahn's study, described in Chapter 6, it would appear that before the advent of the women's movement in the 1960s, women who had achieved an identity involving ca-

reer and motherhood all had fathers who in their affection-
ate relationships with their daughters encouraged and
supported their achievements. This included fathers who
allowed their daughters to identify with their own accomplishments and efforts to succeed and compete. As Bernstein points out, to the extent that fathers feel threatened
in their own masculinity, or need to define themselves by
seeing women as inferior, they can discourage efforts to
achieve in their daughters, thus making career involvement
more difficult. A variation on this is cited in a paper by Ruth
Lax[11] where fathers in traditional familes are very encouraging to their daughter's self-assertion and accomplishments, but convey that their love relationship would only
be with a traditional housewife-mother in an inferior position. This results in a split in the woman's psyche where
success is experienced as precluding love relationships,
and love relationships have to be without equality or respect, or even on a sadomasochistic basis, if denigrating
maternal attitudes toward her daughter as a female are also
in the picture.

We have now discussed a number of major factors that
go into an identity synthesis: historical traditions, cultural
norms, social role expectations and opportunities, and a
variety of inner psychological identity elements from childhood and adolescence. Crucial to the realization of any
adult identity is the ongoing mirroring, or social supports
and recognition that an individual experiences. Only highly
unusual individuals can evolve an identity completely tran-
scending their times. The very fact that many women can
have both a career and children today is due to changes in
the social structure brought about by increased education
and work opportunities, and then increased consciousness
on women's part. In any new identity integration, particularly one that goes against many of the cultural norms and
past traditions, social supports and recognition become
particularly important.

Perhaps the most crucial support for dual-role identity is the husband-father. On the one hand, his support and satisfaction in his wife's career is of paramount importance, while increased help with the household and child-rearing is also of major significance. Giving increased help around the home and with children can sometimes be a significant threat to many men's identity. Increased involvement with child rearing may tap early unconscious identifications with their own mothers as the main nurturing figure in traditional households. This role may give increased satisfaction to some men, but for others it threatens their sense of masculinity—they unconsciously experience themselves as being too much like their mothers. As Bernstein points out, heretofore men's needs for nurturing were often vicariously lived out through the wife, as the wife vicariously experienced her strivings for achievement through the husband. However, nurturance as a normal aspect of masculine identity must gradually become a crucial cultural norm, especially for families where the woman has a dual-role identity. Undoubtedly, as sons experience fathers who are much more involved in raising them, they will feel much more comfortable with a nurturing role as an aspect of their masculinity. A further aspect of man's changing role discussed by Jane Lazarre (Chapter 8) and Doris Bernstein (Chapter 5) is that he becomes less a son to his wife, thereby giving up certain demands to be catered to and being more able to fulfill a variety of needs himself—just as the wife becomes less dependent on the husband for decision-making and initiative. Undoubtedly, these changing roles and relationships in marriage have resulted in increased strains. On the other hand, to the extent they can be worked out, a richer life is offered to both men and women.

Support systems and mirroring for dual-role identity extend beyond the family and imply new kinds of institutional and other role patterns and expectations. New

changes in identity and roles call for institutional alterations, as well as profound changes in sociocultural ideals
and career patterns. With regard to the former, as Barbara
Harris points out in Chapter 1, it is clear that a mother with
young children, however committed to her career, simply
cannot devote the time and energy to it that most men can
and do. The career woman should not be penalized professionally for being a mother. Other career women wish to
spend considerable time with their children, especially
when they are very young. At present, only a small number
of professions, such as being a university professor or a
psychotherapist, allow this. It would not only be highly
desirable for a number of other professions and careers to
permit the woman to work part-time if she desires when she
is a mother, but to continue some of the normal benefits
accorded to a full-time person. We do not believe that
interruption of a career is a feasible solution for many
women; interruption usually puts a woman at a great disadvantage in her profession, and often frustrates her as well,
if she is at home all day. Working in a satisfactory career
often increases women's pleasure in their roles as mothers.

In response to cultural ideals and social patterns, many
women adopt the inherently frustrating ideals of being
both supermothers and superprofessionals. On the one
hand, they often cannot spend quite as much time with
their children as they might like; on the other, they do not
have the time or energy to do all that they feel they should
and would like to do in their careers. We believe the solution is to formulate a new cultural ideal that recognizes that
managing both career and motherhood together adds a
whole new dimension to the personality that is not present
when one is either a professional or a mother. The new
whole is greater than the sum of its parts; combining both
roles adds something new to the woman as well as to her
career and her mothering. Furthermore, as this ideal is
more widely accepted and clearly delineated and ways of
practically working out a dual-role identity develop, there

will be less of the ambiguity and conflict that Epstein describes in the current combination of these roles.[12]

As we contemplate the advantages of women combining child-rearing with careers, and the need for institutional alterations of role expectations and patterns, it gradually becomes apparent that many middle-class men could also benefit from a broadening of their own identity in terms of self-fulfillment. How many men are caught up in careers and professions that become so demanding that they not only have little time left over to participate in their families, but also leave other important potentialities undeveloped? Perhaps, here also, there is a need for a reformulation of sociocultural ideals calling for a broadening and combining of roles into a new identity.

Finally, there is the issue of child care, an essential support for the career-involved mother. The extended family is, and always has been, uncommon in the United States, especially among the middle classes, with only rare exceptions among some Eastern European families where the grandparents participate in child rearing while the mothers may have a career. In Chapter 1, Barbara Harris discusses a variety of solutions, from housekeepers to quality child-care centers, hopefully state supported, to greatly increased participation by the husband. Here, too, there are new innovations in social roles taking place to give the needed support for this new identity. One of the more innovative and creative solutions involves cooperative baby-sitting and preschool play groups, where a number of couples get together, partially recreating the extended family. In this particular solution, both men and women participate in child-rearing and wives receive much support in their careers. We are sure that as more women become involved in career and motherhood, other innovative efforts will change institutionalized and noninstitutionalized attitudes and social patterns to render the necessary support for this new identity.

NOTES

CHAPTER 1

[1] U. S. Department of Labor, Bureau of Labor Statistics, *Families and the rise of working wives—an overview,* Special Labor Force Report 189, Reprinted from the *Monthly Labor Review* (May 1976). P. 13. U. S. Department of Labor, Employment Standards Administration, Women's Bureau, *1975 Handbook of women workers,* Bulletin 297. Pp. 18, 26.

[2] U. S. Department of Labor, Employment Standards Administration, Women's Bureau, *The earnings gap between women and men,* 1976. P. 1.

[3] *1975 Handbook of women workers.* P. 137.

[4] In 1968 only 6% of mothers between the ages of 14 and 24 and 8% of mothers between the ages of 30 and 44 used schools or group care facilities for their preschool-age children. Ibid. P. 35. Suzanne H. Woolsey, Pied piper politics and the child-care debate. *Daedalus,* Spring 1977, **106** (2), 127–145.

[5] Jesse Bernard reports that a larger proportion of the children of college-educated women are enrolled in preschools than the children of less well-educated women. Bernard, Jesse. *The future of motherhood.* New York: The Dial Press, 1974. P. 281n. I am sure a major factor here is money.

[6]For those who are wondering about Clifford, his after-school tantrum was a once-in-a-lifetime event, never, thank goodness, repeated. He is now 10, alive, well, and living in Brooklyn.

[7]Bernard. Future of motherhood. P. 204. Rapaport, Rhona, & Rapaport, Robert. The dual career family, a varient pattern and social change. In Constantina Safilios-Rothschild (Ed.), *Toward a sociology of women.* Lexington, Mass.: Xerox College Publishing, 1972. Pp. 226–227.

[8]Garland, T. Neal. The better half? The male in the dual profession family. Ibid. Pp. 199–215.

[9]Lopate, Carol. Marriage and medicine. In Athena, Theodore (Ed.), *The professional woman.* Cambridge, Mass: Schenkman Publishing Co., 1971. Pp. 503–504.

[10]Mainardi, Pat. The politics of housework. In Robin Morgan (Ed.), *Sisterhood is powerful.* New York: A Vintage Book, 1970. Pp. 447–453.

[11]*The Spokeswoman*, April 15, 1977, P. 6.

CHAPTER 2

[1]Freud's one use of the term identity was in reference to himself as a Jew in an address to the B'nai B'rith in Vienna.

[2]Erikson, Erik. *Identity, youth & crisis.* New York: W. W. Norton, 1965.

[3]Freud, Anna. *Collected works.* New York: International Universities Press, 1974. Jacobson, Edith. *The self and the object world.* New York: International Universities Press, 1964. Mahler, Margaret, Pine, Fred, & Bergman, Anni. *The psychological birth of the human infant.* New York: Basic Books, 1975. Segal, Hanna. *Introduction to the work of Melanie Klein.* New York: Basic Books, 1964.

[4]Bernstein, Doris. Childhood identity synthesis. In Alan Roland (Ed.), *Identity, identification, and self-image, psychoanalytic monographs, I.* New York: National Psychological Association for Psychoanalysis, 1971.

CHAPTER 3

[1]Historians often call the cult of domesticity the cult of true womanhood. Welter, Barbara. The cult of true womanhood, 1820–60. *American Quarterly,* Summer 1966, **XVIII**, 151–174. The phrases will be used interchangeably in this chapter.

[2]Hunt, Harriot. *Glances and glimpses.* New York: Source Books Press, 1970. P. 20.

[3]Dexter, Elisabeth. *Colonial women of affairs: women in business and the professions in America before 1776.* Boston: Houghton Mifflin, 1931. Spruill, Julia Cherry. *Women's life and work in the southern colonies.* New York: Norton Library, 1972. Chapters XI–XIV.

[4]Mary P. Ryan does this at points in her recent work, *Womanhood in America.* New York: New Viewpoints, 1975. Chapters 2–3.

[5]Spruill, *Women's life and work.* Pp. 241–242

[6]Dexter, Elisabeth. *Career women of America, 1776–1840.* Francestown, N.H.: Marshall Jones Company, 1950. Pp. 219–225.

[7]Demos, John. American family in past time. *American Scholar,* Summer 1974, **43**, 433–435. Lerner, Gerda. The lady and the mill girl. *Midcontinent American Studies Journal,* Spring 1969, **X**, 5–15.

[8]Jewett, Sarah Orne. The courting of Sister Wisby. In Gail Parker (Ed.), *The oven birds, American women on womanhood, 1820–1920.* Garden City, N.Y.: Doubleday, 1972. Pp. 217–233.

[9]Smith-Rosenberg, Carroll. Beauty, the beast and the militant woman: a case study in sex roles and social stress in Jacksonian America. *American Quarterly,* October 1971, **XXIII** (4), 570–575. Pivar, David J. *Purity crusade.* Westport, Conn.: Greenwood Press, Inc., 1973. passim. Hunt. *Glances and glimpses.* Pp. 107–110, 145–148.

[10]Hunt. *Glances and glimpses.* P. 108.

[11]Ibid. P. 148. Anthony, Susan B. Social purity. In Aileen S. Kraditor (Ed.), *Up from the pedestal.* Chicago: Quadrangle Books, 1968. Pp. 159–167. Smith-Rosenberg. Beauty, the beast and the militant woman. Pp. 574–575, 579–580.

[12]Deger, Carl. What ought to be and what was: Women's sexuality in the nineteenth century. *American Historical Review,* December 1974, **79** (5), 1467–1490.

[13]Recent writers who agree with me without ignoring the existence of other attitudes toward sexuality are Gorden, Michael. From an unfortunate necessity to a cult of mutual orgasm: Sex in American marital education literature. In James M. Henslin (Ed.), *Studies in the sociology of sex.* New York: Appleton-Century-Crofts, 1971. Pp. 53–77. Haller, John, & Haller, Robin. *The physician and sexuality in Victorian America.* Urbana, Ill.: University of Illinois, 1974. Chapter 3. Rosenberg,

Charles E. Sexuality, class and role in nineteenth-century America. *American Quarterly*, May 1973, **25** (2), 131–153.

[14]McGovern, James. The American woman's pre-World War I freedom in manners and morals. *Journal of American History*, 1968, **55**, 315–333. Robinson, Paul. *The modernization of sex: Havelock Ellis, Alfred Kinsey, William Masters and Virginia Johnson*. New York: Harper Torchbook, 1976.

[15]Flexner, Eleanor. *Century of struggle, the woman's rights movement in the United States*. New York: Athenum Books, 1971. P. 26.

[16]Hunt, *Glances and glimpses*. P. 104.

[17]Quoted in Dexter, *Career women of America, 1776–1840*. P. 45.

[18]Houghton, Walter E. *The Victorian frame of mind*. New Haven, Conn.: Yale University Press, 1957. Pp. 356–357. Haller, John S., Jr., & Haller, Robin M. *The physician and sexuality in Victorian America*. Urbana, Ill.: University of Illinois, 1974. Pp. 102–104.

[19]Kemble, Frances Anne. *Journal of a residence on a Georgian plantation in 1839*. New York: Alfred A. Knopf, 1961. Pp. 14, 21.

[20]Trollope, Frances. *Domestic manners of the Americans*. London: Folio Society, 1974. Pp. 120–122.

[21]de Tocqueville, Alexis. *Democracy in America*. New York: Vintage Books, 1945. Vol. II. Third Book. Chapters IX–X.

[22]Houghton, *The Victorian mind*. Chapter 13, part 2, especially pp. 350–351; quotation from p. 351.

[23]Morgan, Edmund. *The Puritan family*. New York: Harper Torchbook, 1966. Chapter 2. Schüking, Levin L. *The Puritan family*. New York: Schocken, 1966. Section 1. Morgan, Edmund. The Puritans and sex. In Michael Gordon (Ed.), *American family in social-historical perspective*. New York: St. Martin's Press, 1973. Pp. 282–295. Haller, William. Hail wedded love. *Journal of English Literary History*, 1946, **13**, 79–96. Demos, John. *A little commonwealth, family life in Plymouth Colony*. New York: Oxford University Press, 1973. Pp. 92, 95–96, 152–153. As Perry Miller has pointed out, most seventeenth-century Englishmen shared Puritan views on most subjects. In this sense, Puritanism should be seen as the most complete and self-conscious definition of Protestantism in English-speaking culture. Caution should be exercised about drawing too great a distinction between Puritanism and Anglicanism in this period since they shared many values and attitudes common to all varieties of Protestantism.

[24]Stone, Lawrence. *Crisis of the aristocracy.* Oxford: Clarendon Press, 1965. Chapter XI, especially pp. 596–600, 610–612, 669–671. Morgan. *Puritan family.* Pp. 78–86. Spruill. *Women's life and work.* P. 143. Walzer, Michael. *Revolution of the saints.* Cambridge: Harvard University Press, 1965. Pp. 193–194.

[25]Osborne, Dorothy. *The letters of Dorothy Osborne to Sir William Temple 1652–54,* edited by Kingsley Hart. London: The Folio Society, 1968, passim.

[26]Hutchinson, Lucy. *Memoirs of the life of Colonel Hutchinson,* Edited by James Sutherland. New York: Oxford University Press, 1973. P. 33.

[27]Morgan. Puritans and sex. P. 284–285.

[28]Ibid. Pp. 285–293. Oberholzer, Emil, Jr. *Delinquent saints.* New York: Columbia University Press, 1956. Pp. 127–151.

[29]Trevor-Roper, Hugh. The general crisis of the seventeenth century. In Trevor Aston (Ed.), *Crisis in Europe 1560–1660.* London: Routledge and Kegan Paul, 1965. Pp. 80–83. Stone. *Crisis of the aristocracy.* Pp. 662–668.

[30]Stone. *Crisis of the aristocracy.* Pp. 596–600, 610–612, 669–671.

[31]Hill, Christopher. Clarissa Harlowe and her times. In *Puritanism and revolution.* London: Mercury Books, 1962. P. 368. Habbakuk, H. J. Marriage settlements in the eighteenth century. *Transactions of the Royal Historical Society,* Fourth Series, 1950, **XXXII**, 24–29. Habbakkuk, H. J. English landownership 1680–1740. *Economic History Review,* 1940, X, 2–17.

[32]Stone. *Crisis of the aristocracy.* Pp. 612, 662–664, 669–671.

[33]Saville, George. Marquess of Halifax. The lady's new year's gift; or, advice to a daughter. In J. P. Kenyon (Ed.), *Complete Works.* Baltimore: Pelican Classics, 1969. P. 279.

[34]Thomas, Keith. The double standard. *Journal of the History of Ideas,* April 1959, **XX** (2), 216.

[35]Ibid. P. 216.

[36]Ibid. Pp. 212–213.

[37]For this and above paragraph see, Watt, Ian. *Rise of the novel.* Berkeley, Calif.: University of California Press, 1964. Pp. 155–162. Hill. Clarissa Harlowe and her times. Pp. 367–394.

[38]Spruill. *Women's life and work.* Pp. 136–137.

[39]Ibid. Pp. 143–147, 172–177.

[40]Ibid. Chapter X.

[41]Welter, Barbara. The feminization of American religion, 1800–60. In Mary Hartman & Lois Banner (Eds.), *Clio's consciousness raised.* New York: Harper Torchbook, 1974. Pp. 137–157, especially 151.

[42]Smith-Rosenberg, Carroll. Beauty, the beast, and the militant woman. Pp. 562–584.

[43]Ariès, Philippe. *Centuries of childhood, a social history of family life.* New York: Vintage, 1962. Stone. *Crisis of the aristocracy.* Pp. 590, 592–593. Hunt, David. *Parents and children in history.* New York: Harper Torchbooks, 1972. Pp. 100–109.

[44]Laslett, Peter. *The world we have lost.* New York: Scribners, 1965. Pp. 45–46, 69–70. Demos, John. *Little commonwealth.* Pp. 57–58, 140.

[45]A description of England in an early Italian relation. In Williams, C. H. (Ed.), *English historical documents.* New York: Oxford University Press, 1967. Vol. V, P. 196.

[46]Wilson, Violet A. *Society women of Shakespeare's time.* Port Washington, N.Y.: Kennikat Press, 1970. P. 66.

[47]Morgan. *Puritan family.* Pp. 75–78. Demos. *Little commonwealth.* Pp. 71–75.

[48]Spruill. *Women's life and work.* Pp. 57–59.

[49]Demos. *Little commonwealth.* Pp. 142–144.

[50]Hunt. *Parents and children.* Pp. 171–173.

[51]Schüking. *The Puritan family.* Pp. 85–88.

[52]Morgan. *Puritan family.* Chapters I, VI. Walzer. *Revolution of the saints.* Pp. 190–193.

[53]Demos. *Little commonwealth.* Pp. 134–139.

[54]Frost, J. William. *The Quaker family in colonial America.* New York: St. Martin's Press, 1973. Pp. 75–79.

[55]Rosenberg, Rosalind Navin. *The dissent from Darwin, 1890–1930: The new view of woman among American social scientists.* Unpublished doctoral dissertation, Stanford University, August 1974. Chapter 1, especially pp. 7–18. The ideas attributed to Darwin come from the *Descent of man* and are not the work of later Darwinists. *Descent of man.* London: first edition, 1871, Random House Modern Library Edition. n.d. Pp. 415, 446–447, 579–584, 873–874, 899, 903.

[56]Chafe, William Henry. *The American woman 1920–1970.* New York: Oxford University Press, 1972. Pp. 58, 60.

[57]Graham, Patricia Albjerg. Women in academe. In Athena, Theodore (Ed.), *The professional woman.* Cambridge, Mass.: Schenkman Publishing Co. Inc., 1971. P. 720–721.

[58]Chafe. *American woman.* Pp. 58–60.

[59]Wilson, Edmund. *Upstate.* New York: Farrar, Straus and Giroux, 1971. Pp. 60–61.

[60]O'Neill, William. *The woman movement.* Chicago: Quadrangle Books, 1971, P. 170.

[61]Newcomer, Mabel. *A century of higher education for American women.* New York: Harpers, 1959. Pp. 211–212. Degler, Carl. Revolution without ideology: the changing place of women in America. In Robert Lifton (Ed.), *The woman in America.* Boston: Beacon Press, The Daedalus Library, 1965. P. 206. Chafe. *American woman.* P. 100.

[62]Rossi, Alice. *Feminist papers.* New York: Bantam Books, 1974. Pp. 328–329.

[63]O'Neill. *The woman movement.* P. 42.

[64]Lasch, Christopher, & Taylor, William R. Two kindred spirits: Sorority and family in New England, 1839–48. *New England Quarterly,* March 1963, **XXXVI** (I), 23–41. Demos. The American family in past time. Pp. 536–538. Smith-Rosenberg, Carroll. The female world of love and ritual: relations between women in nineteenth-century America. *Signs,* Autumn 1975, **I** (1) 1–29.

[65]Rousmaniere, J. Cultural hybrid in the slums: college woman and the settlement house, 1884–94. *American Quarterly,* Spring 1970, **XXII,** 45–66.

[66]Schneir, Miriam (Ed.). *Feminism: the essential historical writings.* New York: Vintage, 1972. P. xvii.

[67]The interpretation of the suffrage movement in this and the following paragraphs is stated most extensively in Kraditor, Aileen. *The ideas of the woman suffrage movement.* 1890–1920. Garden City, N.Y.: Anchor Books, 1971. Although I agree with her thesis that the movement became more conservative and relied increasingly on arguments of expediency, I think the contrast between the first and second generation of feminists is often overstated. Even in her own day, Elizabeth Cady Stanton was more radical intellectually than most of the other pioneers in the movement. Furthermore, despite her reliance on en-

lightenment philosophy in the Seneca Falls Declaration and other pronouncements, she also asserted woman's special maternal nature in her autobiography and other writings. See for example, The matriarchate, in Aileen Kraditor (Ed.), *Up from the pedestal.* Pp. 140–147. On occasion, she used this conviction to argue for giving females the vote. Even racist arguments for woman's suffrage appeared among the first generation, particularly during the struggle for the fourteenth and fifteenth amendments. Blackwell, Henry. What the South can do. In Aileen Kraditor (Ed.), *Up from the pedestal.* Pp. 253–257. Stanton, Elizabeth Cady, Anthony, Susan B., & Gage, Matilda J. The Kansas campaign of 1867. In Rossi (Ed.), *The feminist papers.* Pp. 430–470.

The suffrage movement was more conservative in the last decades of its existence than the woman's rights movement was in the middle of the nineteenth century because it had become large and respectable. It attracted women who would never have joined or supported the woman's movement in the early years when feminists were a tiny, ridiculed minority. As success became a real possibility, the leadership itself became more concerned to defend its program in ideological terms that would command the widest possible support. In the context of late nineteenth-century America, this meant arguing for the vote on the basis of the cult of domesticity or as an expedient measure to defend and improve the American way of life.

Many of the first generation of leaders were still alive and in positions of power when this shift began in the 1870s and 1880s. Their changing emphasis can be attributed to advancing age, disillusionment with the abolitionists and blacks after the fight over the fourteenth and fifteenth amendments, or a decision (conscious or unconscious) to narrow their aims and ideology in order to achieve some success. The longevity of many of the early feminists masked this gradual transition. The only early leader who never accepted the reduction of the woman's movement to pursuit of the vote and who remained an intellectual maverick was Elizabeth Cady Stanton. The suffrage organization formally disavowed her when she published the *Woman's Bible* in 1896. The rise of new leaders in the 1890s and first decades of the twentieth century made the change in the woman's movement much more apparent, but there was never a sharp break that can be easily connected to a generational change in the leadership.

[68]Dubois, Ellen. The radicalism of the woman suffrage movement: notes toward the reconstruction of nineteenth-century feminism. *Feminist Studies,* Fall 1975, **III** (1/2), 65.

[69]Rosenberg. *Dissent from Darwinism.* Pp. 47–51, 57.

[70]O'Neill, William. *Everyone was brave.* Chicago: Quadrangle Paperback, 1971. Pp. 312–313.

[71]Ibid. P. 313. Kennedy, David. *Birth control in America.* New Haven, Conn.: Yale University Press, 1970. Chapter 5.

[72]This interpretation of Freud's ideas about women is based primarily on three of his late essays on the subject: Some psychical consequences of the anatomical distinction between the sexes (1925), in *The Standard Edition of the Complete Psychological Works of Sigmund Freud,* edited by James Stratchey. London: Hogarth Press, 1961. Vol. 19, Pp. 248–258. Female sexuality (1931). Ibid. Vol. 21. Pp. 225–243; Psychology of women, (1933). In *New introductory lectures on psychoanalysis.* New York: W. W. Norton & Co., 1933. Pp. 153–185. I provide citations for specific views attributed to Freud only in cases where I think my interpretation is particularly controversial.

[73]Psychology of women. Pp. 176–177. The passing of the oedipus complex. In Joan Riviere (Ed.), *Collected papers.* New York: Basic Books, 1959. Vol. 2. Pp. 274–275.

[74]Psychology of women. Pp. 179–180. "Civilized" sexual morality and modern nervous illness 1908. In *The standard edition.* Vol. 9. P. 192. In the latter essay Freud explicitly states that woman "possesses a weaker sexual instinct."

[75]Psychology of women. Pp. 183–184. "Civilized" sexual morality. P. 195. Civilization and its discontents, *The standard edition,* Vol. 21, P. 103 refers to "instinctual sublimations of which women are little capable" but does not give any reasons for this incapacity.

[76]Civilization and its discontents. Pp. 103–104.

[77]"Civilized" sexual morality. Pp. 198–199, Psychology of women. Pp. 172–173, Female sexuality. Pp. 229–230, 232 for repression of sexuality as one female response to the discovery of her organic inferiority. Some psychological consequences of the anatomical distinction between the sexes. In James Stratchey, (Ed.), *Collected papers.* New York: Basic Books, 1959. Vol. 5. Pp. 193–194.

[78]Psychology of women. Pp. 157–158, 179–180.

[79]Sinclair, Andrew. *The emancipation of the American woman.* New York: Harper Colophon Books, 1965. Chapter xxxi. Friedan, Betty. *The feminine mystique.* New York: Dell, 1963.

[80]See, for example, Lundberg, Ferdinand, & Farnham, Marynia F. *Modern woman: the lost sex.* New York: Harper & Brothers Publishers, 1947.

CHAPTER 4

[1]Rank, Otto. *Beyond psychology.* New York: Dover, 1958. P. 254.

[2]It should be pointed out that a similar burden of guilt falls on the man who has rejected his father as an ego-ideal. In the case of both men and women it is the parent of the same sex who represents the primary role model and whose rejection is therefore most crucial in the creation of guilt feelings—not only for deviation from the parent figure, but for disloyalty to a part of oneself.

[3]Menaker, Esther, & Menaker, William. *Ego in evolution.* New York: Grove Press, 1965.

CHAPTER 5

[1]Hartmann, Heinz. *Ego psychology and the problem of adaptation.* New York: International Universities Press, 1958. Erikson, Erik H. *Childhood and society.* New York: W. W. Norton, 1950. Menaker, Esther, & Menaker, William. *Ego in evolution.* New York: Grove Press, 1965.

[2]Broverman, Inge K., Broverman, Donald M., Clarkson, Frank E., Rosenkrantz, Paul S., & Vogel, Susan R. Sex role stereotypes and clinical judgments of mental health. *Journal of Consulting and Clinical Psychology,* 1970, **34,** 1–7.

[3]Mahler, Margaret S. *On human symbiosis and the vicissitudes of individuation.* New York: International Universities Press, 1968.

[4]Awareness of oneself as male or female.

[5]Stoller, Robert J. On the development of masculinity and femininity. In *Sex and gender.* Vol. I. New York: Jason Aronson, 1968.

[6]Weil, Edmund. The origin and the vicissitudes of the self-image. *Psychoanalysis and the Psychoanalytic Review.* 1958, **6,** 3–19. Jacobson, Edith. *The self and the object world.* New York: International Universities Press, 1964. Mahler, *On human symbiosis.*

[7]If I were to venture a hypothesis, I would say that part of the mother's relationship to the girl is a reflection of the mother's early narcissism (i.e., narcissism on the undifferentiated level). Jacobson, *Self and the object world.* The mother's revived narcissism from her own symbiotic stage is quite different from the narcissism she experiences at a later stage in her development. The narcissism that appears in relation to her son is a reflection of that later state. It is more object-oriented; the son is viewed as her phallic or anal treasure (object) instead of as part of herself.

[8]Stoller. *Sex and gender*. P. 263.

[9]The ego develops out of a mental representation of the child's discovery and experience of his or her own body.

[10]Roiphe, Herman. On an early genital phase: With an addendum on genesis. *Psychoanalytic Study of the Child*, 1968, **23**, 348–365.

[11]For example, women's cognition has been described as being more "intuitive," from a sense or feeling toward the cognitive statement. Men's cognition is described as the reverse; the clear logical thought followed by inner reverberations.

[12]Freud, Sigmund. Dissolution of the Oedipus complex. In *Standard edition*. Vol. 19. Pp. 173–179.

[13]Applegarth, Adrienne. Some observations in work inhibitions in women. *Journal of American Psychoanalytic Association*. Supplement: Female Psychology, 1976, **24**, 251–268.

[14]Freud, Sigmund. Group psychology and the analysis of the ego. *Standard edition*. Vol. 18. Pp. 69–143.

[15]Reich, Annie. Early identifications as archaic elements in the superego. *Journal of American Psychoanalytic Association*, 1954, **2**, 218–238.

[16]Freud, Sigmund. Some psychical consequences of the anatomical distinctions between the sexes. In *Standard edition*. Vol. 19. Pp. 248–258.

[17]Spitz, René A. *No and yes—on the genesis of human communication*. New York: International Universities Press, 1957.

[18]Sheehy, Gail. *Passages: Predictable crises of adult life*. New York: E. P. Dutton, 1976.

[19]See also Charlotte Kahn in this volume.

[20]Lax, Ruth. The role of internalization in the development of certain aspects of female masochism: Ego psychological considerations. *International Journal of Psychoanalysis*, 1977, **58** (3), 289–300.

[21]Nagara, Humberto. *Female sexuality and the Oedipus complex*. New York: Jason Aronson, 1975.

[22]Schafer, Roy. Problems in Freud's psychology of women. *Journal of American Psychoanalytic Association*, 1974, **22**, 459–485. Torok, Maria. The significance of penis envy in women. In J. Chasseguet-Smirgel (Ed.), *Female sexuality: New psychoanalytic views*. Ann Arbor: University of Michigan Press, 1970. Pp. 135–170. Chasseguet-Smirgel, J. Feminine guilt and the Oedipus complex. In ibid. Pp. 94–134.

CHAPTER 6

[1]This selection was presented in its original form to the Institute for Psychoanalytic Training and Research at its meeting on November 29, 1973, at the New York Academy of Science. I am indebted to Dr. Margaret Ray for her encouragement and especially for her help in elaborating the concept of fusion of identifications.

[2]Deutsch, Helene. *The psychology of women.* New York: Grune & Stratton, 1944. Vol. 1, P. 247.

[3]Schneider, Lynn R. The relationship between identification with mother and home or career orientation. Unpublished doctoral dissertation, Columbia University, 1962.

[4]Deutsch. *The psychology of women.* Pp. 250, 253.

[5]Ibid. P. 269.

[6]Ibid. P. 361.

[7]Ibid. P. 362.

[8]Sublimation is the unconscious substitution of an acceptable and gratifying activity for an inimicable expression of an unconscious instinctual impulse. For example, excellence in competitive sports may be a substitute for the expression of aggressive impulses through physical assault or murder.

[9]Ibid. P. 227.

[10]Binstock, William A. On the two forms of intimacy. *Journal of the American Psychoanalytic Association,* 1973, **21** (1), 93–107.

CHAPTER 7

[1]This is a psychoanalytic concept used to describe the "average-expectable mother."

[2]Transference is largely made up of the predisposed feelings and fantasies of the individual that are then transferred to the analyst. These distortions of the self and others are then dealt with mainly through interpretation.

[3]Resistances are modes through which the analysand avoids dealing with the crucial dynamic issues.

[4]Defenses are related to resistances and are particular (psychopathological) characterological modes of dealing with psychodynamic issues.

[5]Horner, Mattina. *Sex differences in achievement motivation and performance in competitive and non-competitive situations.* (Doctoral dissertation, University of Michigan) Ann Arbor, Mich.: University Microfilms, 1968. No. 69-12, 135.

[6]Horner, Mattina. Toward an understanding of achievement-related conflicts in women. *Journal of Social Issues,* 1972, **28** (2), 157–175.

[7]McClelland, David C. *Personality.* New York: William Sloane Association, 1951.

[8]Winterbottom, Marian R. The relation of need for achievement to learning experience in independence and mastery. In J. W. Atkinson (Ed.), *Motives in fantasy, action and society.* Princeton, N.J.: D. Van Nostrand, 1958. Pp. 453–478.

[9]Veroff, Joseph. Social comparison and the development of achievement motivation. In C. P. Smith (Ed.), *Achievement related motives in children.* New York: Russell Sage, 1969.

[10]Bardwick, Judith M. *Psychology of women.* New York: Harper & Row, 1971.

[11]Podhoretz, Harriette. *Motivation of female doctoral students: Manifest needs, perceived parenting and locus of control.* Unpublished doctoral dissertation, Fordham University, New York, 1974.

[12]Mahler, Margaret, Pine, Fred, & Bergman, Anni. *The psychological birth of the human infant: Symbiosis and individuation.* New York: Basic Books, 1975.

[13]Jacobson, Edith. *The self and the object world.* New York: International Universities Press, 1964.

[14]This theory views the structure of the unconscious as containing internalized images or representations, that is, of the self and important others such as mother, father, etc. These images and their internal interactions are in a state of constant flux that subtly interact with personal and social relationships, and regulate emotions (e.g., self-esteem).

[15]Mahler's definition of separation-individuation refers to "the intrapsychic achievement of a sense of separateness from mother and through that from the world at large."

[16]Symbiosis is regarded as an early stage of development (neonate through infancy) in which the child does not experience the mother or himself/herself as separate, but as a unit.

[17]The child's developmental period has been roughly divided into two phases or stages, the preoedipal and the oedipal; the former basically concerns the mother-child dyad (0 to 3½ years) and subsumes the impulses and feelings of the oral and anal period as well as symbiosis and separation. The latter is triangular (i.e., child, mother, and father) and marks the unfolding of the phallic (3½ to 6 years), and involves sexual rivalry and competition for the opposite-sexed parent. It should be noted that this differentiation of phases allows for overlapping.

[18]Jacobson. *The self and the object world.* P. 83.

[19]Ibid. P. 83.

[20]Ibid. P. 83.

[21]Ibid. P. 84.

[22]Ibid. P. 91.

[23]The negotiation of this stage will determine the girl's later love choice (e.g., as to whether she selects an approving, encouraging, and admiring mate or one who restricts and prohibits her self-actualization).

[24]Whereas for men, anxiety about superseding father would tend to inhibit self-actualization.

[25]As a result of eating binges, she also suffered from overweight.

CHAPTER 8

[1]Juhasz, Suzanne, *Naked and fiery forms: Modern American poetry by women: A new tradition.* New York: Harper & Row, 1976. From Introduction: The Double Bind of the Woman Poet.

[2]Woolf, Virginia. *To the lighthouse.* New York: Harcourt, Brace and World, 1955. P. 223.

[3]Olsen, Tillie. Silences: When writers don't write. Reprinted from a talk given at Radcliffe Institute for Independent Study, by *Harpers Magazine,* October 1965, p. 153.

[4]Moore, Honor. Wrap-around on motherhood. *Harper's Weekly,* June 14, 1976.

[5]Sarton, May. *Mrs. Stevens hears the mermaid singing.* New York: W. W. Norton and Co., 1965.

[6]The trickster is a pervasive character in American Indian mythology, the ambiguous creator and destroyer, subhuman and superhuman, the

concrete symbol of an archetypal aspect of the human psyche. See Radin, Paul. *The trickster, a study in American Indian mythology,* with commentaries by Karl Kerenyi and C. G. Jung and introduction by Stanley Diamond. Republished in 1972 by Schocken Books, New York.

[7]Rich, Adrienne. *Of woman born.* New York: W. W. Norton and Co. 1976. P. 225.

[8]Juhasz, *Naked and fiery forms.* Chapter 5. The blood jet, the poetry of Sylvia Plath.

[9]Quoted by Tillie Olsen in Silences. P. 156.

[10]Ibid. P. 160.

[11]Olsen, Tillie. *I stand here ironing.* In Susan Cahill (Ed.), *Women and fiction.* New York: Mentor, New American Library, 1975. P. 166.

[12]Rich, *Of woman born.* P. 209.

[13]Ibid. P. 191.

CHAPTER 9

[1]Friedan, Betty. *The feminine mystique.* New York: Dell Publishing, 1963.

[2]Ibid.

[3]Ryan, Mary P. *Womanhood in America.* New York: New Viewpoints, 1975. Pp. 305–361. Chafe, William Henry. *The American woman, 1920–1970.* New York: Oxford University Press, 1972. Parts Two and Three. Millet, Kate. *Sexual politics.* New York: Avon Books, 1970. Part II.

[4]Rank, Otto. *Art and the artist.* New York: Knopf, 1932. Menaker, Esther, & Menaker, William. *Ego in evolution.* New York: Grove Press, 1965. Erikson, Erik. *Identity, youth, and crisis.* New York: W. W. Norton, 1965. Maslow, Abraham. *The farther reaches of human nature.* New York: Viking Press, 1971. Angyal, Andrus, *Neurosis and treatment: A holistic theory.* New York: John Wiley & Sons, 1965. Fromm, Erich. *Man for himself.* New York: Rinehart & Co., 1947. White, Robert W. *Ego and reality in psychoanalytic theory, psychological issues. Monograph II.* New York: International Universities Press, 1963. Rogers, Carl. *Becoming partners: Marriage and its alternatives.* New York: Delacorte Press, 1972. Rogers, Carl. *On becoming a person.* Boston: Houghton Mifflin, 1961.

[5]Abraham Maslow mentioned this anecdote in a lecture at Cooper Union in the late 1950s.

[6]Hartmann, Heinz. *Ego psychology and the problem of adaptation.* New York: International Universities Press, 1958.

[7]Applegarth, Adrienne. Some observations in work inhibitions in women. *Journal of American Psychoanalytic Association.* Supplement: Female Psychology, 1976, **24,** 251–268.

[8]Winnicott, D. W. *The maturational process and the facilitating environment.* New York: International Universities Press, 1965. Spitz, René. *The first year of life.* New York: International Universities Press, 1965. Kohut, Heinz. *The analysis of the self.* New York: International Universities Press, 1973. Mahler, Margaret, Pine, Fred, & Bergman, Anni. *The psychological birth of the human infant.* New York: Basic Books, 1975.

[9]Rossi, Alice. A biosocial perspective on parenting. *Daedalus,* Spring 1977.

[10]Menaker, Esther, & Menaker, William. *Ego in evolution.* New York: Grove Press, 1965.

[11]Lax, Ruth. The role of internalization in the development of certain aspects of female masochism: Ego psychological considerations. *International Journal of Psychoanalysis,* 1977, **58** (3), 289–300.

[12]Epstein, Cynthia Fuchs. *Women's place.* Berkeley, Calif.: University of California Press, 1970.

INDEX

DATE DUE